home ♥ love

For Giles,
who puts the love into home.

megan morton

home ♥ love

100 inspiring ideas
for creating beautiful rooms

LANTERN
an imprint of
PENGUIN BOOKS

contents

attention to detail

getting down to brass tacks

but wait, there's more

introduction

Spending my formative years on a banana farm in Queensland really gave my imagination lots of scope. Ours was a desolate family home in terms of decoration (but super-fun in terms of family life!). For colour I was left with not much more than the bananas (hence my general love for yellow) and beautiful clear blue sunny skies.

I'm convinced that keen observation might be the best attribute for a designer or stylist, and I have the same excited feelings now about redecorating my room as I did as a wide-eyed child. I'm also convinced that sharing is the best way to keep the world beautiful, as there is no point keeping it all to yourself! I'm a firm believer that when you're willing to share what you know, others share with you – it's the power of karmic knowledge.

There are dozens of decorating lessons in this book, some of which originally appeared in my *Sydney Morning Herald/The Age* 'Good Weekend' column 'DIY Home', but I couldn't stand the thought of dishing out old words, so I've added lots to each. Some of the other lessons are brand new, and cover topics I just had to write about (such as 'Hanging with the French' on page 112).

I write not only as a design professional and a stylist but also as someone who shares their home with three children (by the time HOME LOVE appears), a husband and a schnauzer. I love the indecently beautiful as well as the practical, and I believe that beautiful rooms are rarely accidental. Logic always underpins their success – along with the alignment of lots of decorative stars. I treat rooms with a very black-and-white attitude, and find that in my line of work there isn't a lot of room for 'grey' (unless it's a wall colour – Bauwerk 20/20, please!). So whether you're living solo in an apartment or decorating the family home, if you do it with conviction, you've taken a step in the right direction. I love making rooms with all my heart and dedicate this book to every stylist, designer and decorator who bring spaces to life.

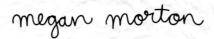

megan morton

meganmorton.com

(For more HOME LOVE, please register for my blog at homelove.blog.com)

rooms for living

Your dream bedroom

The main bedroom is so private that most of us throw all our money into more obvious rooms, such as the living room and kitchen, where we can show off our good taste to as many people as possible. No one really ever comes into the bedroom, unless, of course, they have a personal invitation. It's for this reason alone that we should rethink the way we dress our bedrooms.

Tips for the bedroom? I have so many! You can skimp on lighting, skimp on bedside tables but, whatever you do, don't skimp on your mattress. Considering what a good one costs, I think it's silly they don't let you test-drive them for at least one night. When I grow up, I'm going to buy a mattress from Hästens. Their Vividus bed could be one of the world's most expensive at about AU$60 000, but it's made by hand, filled with horsehair, cotton and flax and there are no words to describe what it feels like to sleep in. (Their website, hastens.com, suggests hotels – none of them in Australia, unfortunately – where you can sleep in one of their distinctive blue-and-white-checked beds.)

If you share a bed with someone who doesn't have, let's say, the same sleeping spirit, I suggest you invest in two blankets and/or doonas to suit you both – or blankets or doonas that have a heavy and a light half. All persuasions are now catered for in doona weights, pillow firmness and blanket compositions. When it comes time to make the bed, one side might look extra puffy, but no one will really be any the wiser.

I've seen many bedrooms that play host to the house's best artwork and I've always felt that this is a real waste – you and your guests will rarely enjoy it there. I would rehang it in the lounge room or dining room to increase its exposure. You can fill the space it leaves in the bedroom with all your personal trinkets, photographs and favourite books.

Tread softly with colours – neutrals are the best way to create a democratic, unisex bedroom. I always feel sorry for men who are forced to sleep in rooms that are all boudoir or super-pretty parlour-style. I did see one example that worked for a couple, though. He wanted super-slick contemporary styling and she wanted colour. He got his way with his modern set-up – at least until you opened the wardrobe doors. She had painted the inners in her section hot pink, and all her gorgeous girly clothes stood out against them to incredible effect. It was a genius idea, given it's a space she gets to experience at least twice a day.

Sleep tight!

Now I'm being super general here, but in my opinion you need a room approximately 5 × 4.5 metres to accommodate a king-sized bed. Any smaller and it's like fitting a square peg into a weeny round hole. I'm tall and married to a fellow tallie, which is the only reason I have a king-sized bed (well, that and the fact that I was never any good at control-crying and so had the children in what became the family bed for a long time). But my room has a 5 × 5 metre floor plan. If I weren't so tall and didn't live with a giant, a queen would be more than adequate. In Sweden, the land of tall people, they never go bigger than a double – except if they buy from Hästens! – and they don't seem to have any trouble in the bedroom department. They would rather save space than block it up with a chunky mattress.

A kitchen for living in

Thanks to the over-advertised phenomenon of the before-and-after kitchen, it seems that there are only two types nowadays: the renovated and the unrenovated. So many of the after kitchens channel showroom perfection, but I feel that this is the one room you can really put your imprint on and make cosy.

As a stylist I get to live vicariously through other people's renovations, so I see which ideas work and which surfaces look good when they're bigger than their chip sample, and I'm privy to how much it sets the owners back. As blessings go, this is a double-edged sword: while I get to handle all the good stuff, there's never any time for me to do my own kitchen when I'm always tinkering with other people's!

I do have a kitchen plan, though. It's a complicated hybrid of all the best ideas I've been lucky enough to witness. The Master Plan, which sits in a folder with plastic sleeves full of drawn-on serviettes, photographs of bench widths and random notes, stands next to My Recipe Folder (see below) in the Unrenovated Kitchen. But it will be *so* lovely when it's done. It will have immaculately clean lines but, due to some deviously clever surface combinations, an inherent sense of charm. Oh, and no implement will have been ignored – there will be a dedicated nook and cranny for every single one of them. I'd also like to hang artwork in mine – a favourite picture that everyone who walks into my house will get to see.

As the backbone of the house, the kitchen deserves as much of your TLC as any other room. If you're fortunate enough to have a large kitchen space, use its scale to handle large elements, such as oversized lights (as seen here), a conversation-piece island bench, bold artwork or brightly coloured cookware. Speaking of colour, I think that white kitchens make a fabulous backdrop for coloured extras, while white elements work their magic in coloured kitchens or against bright splashbacks.

As there are so many components that need to work well within the space, it's a case of figuring out what you will reveal versus what you should conceal. Luckily, thanks to the kitchen-mad climate we live in, there are plenty of options (in every colour) that function well *and* look great.

Slightly exxy but pre-labelled folders, such as My Recipe Book from kikki.K (kikki-k.com.au), are just psychological tools to trick you into making progress. While I love them myself, any old folder will do the trick. We all know, of course, that a prettier folder might help us *want* to do it. kikki.K also sells a fabulous house-reno folder (My Dream Home) – satisfying to look at once the paint has dried! Whatever you use will help put you in control, keep track of expenditure and find the names and numbers of tradespeople.

The hidden kitchen

The popularity of the disappearing kitchen comes as no surprise, given the way we live now and the space constraints most of us are up against. It's a way of sharing space with an adjoining lounge or dining room that allows the cook to be part of the conversation, and can also turn the kitchen into a beautiful backdrop for living. Architect Hannah Tribe, of Sydney's Tribe Studio, sees the trend as a way of reinforcing the overall style of your home. 'The kitchen needs to morph from super-efficient work area to clean living space,' she says. 'Who wants to be reminded of dirty saucepans when they sit down to dinner?'

But if you're considering a hidden kitchen, you should bear in mind the following:

- A kitchen like this relies on perfection – Choose contractors with a record for precise work: near enough is not good enough in these spaces.
- It's easy for open surfaces to get cluttered – This is not a kitchen style that handles knick-knacks: think grand gestures rather than smaller elements.
- Materials are very important given the expanses you're dealing with – Make your decision knowing that a white benchtop will look like an awful lot of white and a long sheet of stainless steel will seem almost preternaturally large. One way to try before you buy is to wrap paper or cardboard the colour of the material you'd like around the unit or area in question.
- Neutrals and whites are your best bet for the open-plan life – Any other option goes against the whole principle of seamless open-plan.
- Don't let the contractor talk you into bull-nosing (rounding off the corners) any surface – It can make them seem very dated.
- If your budget is tight, spend as much as you can on your main tap and stove top – They set the tone for the type of space you create.
- Resist the urge to overuse metallic finishes – A slice, as in this photo, is perfect.
- Think about your overhead cabinet height – You can keep them just shy of the ceiling (the more beautiful option but it creates a dust trap) or you can take them to full height (and accept a bulkier look).
- Design and dress the kitchen with regard to when you'll use it most – Ask yourself if it will look great at breakfast as well as at dinner.

Benchtops are getting higher and higher. I'm tall so mine are 90 centimetres, which is perhaps too high but suits me perfectly. A catering friend who is not tall has his at 1.1 metres! He insists they're fabulous to work from.

Bathroom beautiful

Since a plumber can charge more than a solicitor, most people are forced to work around and within the existing plumbing arrangements when renovating their bathroom. If, however, you like to throw money around on invisible things, then by all means relocate the plumbing. Most bathroom renos are an act of beautification on the surface, allowing the renovator to agonise over basin styles and towel rails. New tapware can improve the spunk of a slightly outdated sink, and a freestanding bath in the space the old fitted one left behind makes for an instant modern upgrade. Enjoy the sleek new lines of a suspended sink from the vantage point of a round-edged tub, and before you know it you won't even notice the not-so-new tiles or the unhinged cabinet door.

There's a wide range of spending categories when it comes to the bathroom: storage, soft furnishings, window treatments, fittings, tapware, toilets – and we haven't even got to the accessories selection. You might be surprised to learn that some tubs are the price of a small car, but bath people don't baulk at bath prices, they just feel sorry for those of us who don't have one.

If you're lucky enough to own a separate bath and shower, dedicate at least one night a week to baths. That way, you'll get to sit back and admire all the beautiful new alterations you've made. Glass apothecary jars, moveable storage, imported soaps and soak powders are all good eye candy that will improve the room the easy way. And then, of course, there are the new towels. Bright colours can distract from the more unsatisfying spaces, while tonal matches with your tiles, surfaces and cabinetry can be simply beautiful. Most of us go for white towels, which is funny considering they're the hardest of all to keep looking their best.

In fact, apart from the fixtures, don't feel that everything in the bathroom must always be white – it's a room that can take some mood, mystery, colour and tonality. Play with woods, paint, brave surfaces and shapes you never thought you'd go for – it's the one safe place you can channel your inner decorator and really get to enjoy the fruits of your labours. I love it when people are brave enough to hang art in their bathrooms. Ross Peck, master framer (rpart.com.au), suggests that, due to steam and moisture issues in the bathroom, we should only hang work there that is reasonably expendable. Oils on stretched canvas are best, because anything under glass or framed might encourage mould.

I'm a plumber's daughter, so my dad gave me the all-time best bathroom advice: 'Honey, it doesn't matter what shape your bathroom's in, always make sure your water pressure's sweet.' Not even the sexiest of shower roses can save us from an underwhelming (or overwhelming) supply of water. If you're beautifying your bathroom, make water pressure your number-one priority before you go tile or tap shopping, and you'll never be disappointed.

For a beautiful bathroom you might need a claw tub, reliable tiles and a good cleaner:

- Grand Slipper – A white claw bath with brass feet from Recollections (recollections.com.au).
- Sand Beige Brushed and Desert – Porcelain tiles from tiletecnics (tiletecnics.com.au).
- Boy's Bathroom Cleaner – From Murchison-Hume (murchison-hume.com. au). They also have the chicest organic cotton shower curtain.

Adding charm to your dining room

Just like people, some rooms have it and others don't, no matter how hard they try. It's that elusive X-factor that visitors to a room can detect the moment they walk in. Some rooms (due to fabulous bones, supermodel-tall ceilings or gorgeous plasterwork) are born with it, while others have to work a little harder, usually at the cost of thousands of renovation dollars. And herein lies the quandary: if you overdose on charm or put in too much effort to create it, you risk stepping into the contrived zone.

The dining room is a great place to practise decorative charm. Given that it plays headquarters to most meals, it's paramount that it retain its practicality. I've seen many winning dining rooms around the styling traps. Some handle the combination of hand-me-down table and modern expensive chairs with aplomb. Others do the exact opposite (brand-new table surrounded by lovely aged chairs) with the same beautiful mixed-marriage result.

I love dining rooms that really make you want to settle in for the night, with chairs that whisper, 'Sit down, I'll make you happy forever,' and a table that's sturdy in both design and service. We've all seen the pretentious dinner table, a place that could be mistaken for a corporate boardroom. Most people like to keep their dining room a sparse service machine, trading on the hunch that people, activity and energy will fill it. I like the idea of having it filled almost to capacity with objects (open storage nooks, piles of my preferred crockery, my best daily-use glassware and, of course, a wine-chiller) so that when we sit down, it's already got a pulse of its own.

It's a high-investment room, so add expensive elements and they should last you a lifetime. Whether it be white soup bowls stacked en masse, a jar full of essentially useless but handsome utensils or just the ultimate in chairs, spoil your dining room – it's the one room that really does give a lot back.

I love how a stack of white bowls can look so humble and yet so stunning. I adore oversized Limoges ones. (I bought them on the roadside from a gypsy caravan in the South of France, so email me if you're going to that part of the world – I have some weird but reliable directions.) I also love Jasper Conran's Wedgwood bowls, and Chinatown cheap-as-chips ones. The more the merrier, I say. I refuse to have one general fruit bowl – instead I make use of my endless stacks of bowls and set up little fruit-stall-like bowls, one full of grapes, another of cherries and so on. Smaller bowls keep you buying fruit more often, so it's always fresher – and fruit isn't particularly attractive anyway when it's all jumbled together! Who wants to look at the 'before' of a fruit salad?

Getting the nursery right first go

What to Expect When You're Expecting really should include a chapter on decorating. You can waste more time and money on this element than on a nappy service. First-time parents often make the mistake of going to town on their baby's room only to discover some sobering facts. First, babies can only see in black and white for the first four months of their lives, so your multicoloured animal wall frieze is a wasted effort. Secondly, creating the room you never had as a baby but feel you should have had is not only sad but probably not a great way to spend your decorating dollars.

There are decorators and designers who exist specifically to help people dress and decorate nurseries and children's rooms and, given their bulging diaries, I can only imagine that, for them, a first-born's room is akin to a first wedding for an events planner. It's big-dollars-spare-no-expense territory.

This is a very long, roundabout way of admitting that I spent way too much time, effort and money on my own daughter's room, a room so over decorated that neither she nor I could stand it when the time came to actually use it. Thanks to cushion overload, it was far too laborious to get her into her over-stuffed bed, and the colour combination of apple green and raspberry red was so contrived and consistent I still can't believe I was its originator.

Babies need very little, but this fact doesn't sit well with our overwhelming desire to feather our nest. When you become a parent, a small part of your brain goes to goo and you decide that it's entirely rational to spend a month's wages on a cot that will house your prince/princess for the first three months of his/her life. Not to mention the matching wardrobe for your precious one's clothes, expensive hangers to go in it and, just for fun, a monogrammed bath towel. Oh dear!

But there's no point telling any of this to someone who's expecting. You'll find yourself popping into all the baby shops 'just to have a look'. The best lesson is this: the minute you admit that you're possibly buying all this fabulous stuff for yourself rather than your offspring, you'll realise you need far less.

For more smart tips on your baby's room, see 'Kitting out the nursery' on page 14.

In the spirit of unisex rooms, here are three boy- and girl-friendly colours:

1. Waterlily – A serene soft grey-green from Murobond (murobond.com.au), with red accessories for a girl and dark grey for a boy.
2. Heartbreaker – A soft lilac from Resene (resene.com.au), with white accessories for a girl and dark grey for a boy.
3. Tasman – A grey from Resene (resene.com.au), with pinkish accessories for a girl and handsome navy for a boy.

Kitting out the nursery

I find the idea of a nursery decorator both indulgent and wildly exciting. Tina de Salis, from boutique firm Tina & Louise, says that the nursery begins and ends with the type of cot you want. The ever-popular multi-use Stokke (stokke-nursery.com) starts off as a cot and ends up as a desk for a nine-year-old. (Divide its price by the number of years of service and you're looking at quite a cost-effective purchase.) Tina did her own daughter's nursery in divine lilac polka dots – great for longevity and an ideal backdrop for Tina's confident use of colour: she worked in hot pink, aqua and teal until baby Bridget's room was picture-perfect.

Decorating aside, a few things are mandatory for a newborn's room:

- Bins – Lots of them. Some for wet waste, some for dry and others for complete burning/tossing/removing. Keep the lids – this room is all about what to reveal versus what to conceal.
- Chair – Don't fall into the trap of choosing a chair for purely aesthetic reasons. An Eames fibreglass chair on a rocker base in powder blue is visual perfection but *not* the best chair in which to breastfeed or nurse your baby to sleep. Neither is an unsightly Jason recliner, but it does combine function and form (only just) once it has a loose cover in a beautiful fabric.
- Fabrics – If only Prada made baby furniture upholstered in their easy-care quilted nylon, upkeep on this room would be easy! Babies' outputs stick to *everything* – like glue, but worse. Avoid anything textural at all costs, unless you like removing gunk from velvet pile with a toothpick. Not the best use of your time.
- Window dressings – Until you know what kind of sleeper your baby is, resist the urge to install intricate block-out curtains unless you absolutely have to. In most cases all you'll need is a decorative curtain. A baby who learns to sleep in pitch black can become one of those annoying adults who can only sleep with the aid of an eye mask and drawn curtains.
- Bed dressing – This is a topic riddled with health risks and SIDS dangers, so please cross-check with a professional and sidsandkids.org. To my mind, though, there's nothing more beautiful than a new baby sleeping in the purest of white sheeting. I bought single adult sheets in the best thread-count cotton I could afford at the time and cut them down into cot sheets, getting two sets from one.

If you're one of those adults who can only sleep with an eye mask and drawn curtains, you must try remogeneralstore.com for their velvet-lined mask.

Accommodating your Little Miss

Unfortunately, there's no set of recognisable warning signs for when your baby girl becomes a Little Miss, no particular age bracket for which you can diarise. And there's nothing you can really do about it, either. Her room, once reserved for just sleeping and storing her adorable little clothes, suddenly becomes her own micro-world and the room – and its contents – really counts. During this phase, it offers full service and comfort, but most of all gives the little lady – your Little Miss – a chance to express herself.

I've witnessed enough hysterical mother–daughter decor wars to know that this is generally the one room to leave be. Don't push too hard one way or the other, or you'll risk outright rebuttal. One of Sydney's most impressive Victorian homes, filled with covetable French antiques, has one room with a different decorative spirit altogether – the daughter's room. It is sparsely dressed in purposeful melamine furniture: the daughter, on her tenth birthday, asked that the antique white-washed armoire be removed in favour of regular built-ins and that the twenty-armed chandelier groaning with crystals and glass butterflies be replaced with simple task-lighting.

Letting your little girl commit decorative anarchy might not seem ideal to you, but the point is to be a little flexible. Many people let their children choose their own paint colour for the walls, but this almost always ends up just plain ugly. I let my own Little Bo Peep do it once, not having researched the maddening effect of true orange. (Colour psychology tells us that orange can energise and agitate. Just my luck!) I'm all for the lovely washed-out powdery colours that are hard to use in general rooms, such as the pale pink Strawberries and Cream by Porter's Paints (porterspaints.com.au) and the powder blue Space by Covered in Paint (coveredinpaint.com.au), but we all know that fuchsia and livid purple are usually more to our Little Misses' taste. If you must let her choose, then limit her colour input to a feature wall or even an inset area that can be repainted in time. I say let them go crazy on the bed linen, lampshades, side tables and desk units – all of which are moveable and replaceable.

Whatever you do, the ideal outcome is a happy young person who feels that their opinion counts. One thing I *do* know: regardless of your budget, your house and your girl, at this age she's blessed with endless energy, creativity and enthusiasm, so you'd be a fool not to put it to use. Get her to do the lion's share of the planning, shopping, research and work.

Or take it one step further – be a real party-pooper and allocate her a decorating budget. Life skills indeed! If only my own mother had done that, things might have turned out differently for me . . .

I do have one general tip: invest in a good-quality king-single mattress (it's actually only 12 centimetres longer than a standard single). It will last her well into her teens, or you can pair it with another in the guest room to replicate a full king-sized bed.

Pleasing an early teen

'Show me a child until he is seven and I will give you the man': this Jesuit saying is the engaging premise of Michael Apted's *Up Series*. I'm convinced that the girl at fourteen is pretty close to her true interior self at thirty-four. Remembering your own fourteenth year might go a long way to explaining your room's status at this moment, and a phone call to your mum will confirm it. My mum attests that I was an abnormally messy teen who considered the floor to be part of my wardrobe. Nothing much has changed: instead of using the floor to store my clothes, I now use a treadmill (well it sure beats exercising).

The one recurring piece of advice I garnered from all the mothers of early teens I spoke to (who use their treadmill for exercise purposes, I also observed) was storage. The theory is that if you provide enough of it, that's pretty much it. 'Just make sure it functions and it's easy to get to. This is all you need to do,' said one, adding, 'Sometimes it's all you *can* do.'

I then took it to the teenagers, and here's what I learnt:

- They'll clean up if given the right tools – This means enough time to tackle the job as well as the necessary implements. Those 'Five minutes to get your room in order or else' ultimatums will more than likely prove counterproductive.
- They like to have some say as to their decor – Let them select colour ways, furniture, a lampshade and rugs if they show interest.
- The close-the-door-and-ignore-it attitude doesn't make a difference – They generally don't suffer from room-indignity as we do.
- Sharing is okay within reason – But each child's personality, and more importantly age group, must be recognised and reflected within the one room.
- Girls don't always want pink, nor boys blue – Same for yellow and purple.
- They like a clean space – It's easier to know where things are and to think clearly in a clean room, but they don't always have the inclination to create one. Be sure to teach them the principles of cause and effect if you want them to learn to keep things tidy.
- They like clever storage – A kitchen cutlery-drawer insert is great for storing jewellery and smaller pieces of technology.
- Be generous on the rubbish facilities – Offer a bin for both dry and wet rubbish.
- They prefer to have their own dirty-clothes hamper – In their own room.
- Cleaning up an entire room can be overwhelming, no matter what your age – They'll appreciate your company and help at times.

Kids can smell a hypocrite a mile away, so it's hard to get them to clean up if you're just as messy. Try to set a good example, otherwise you have no choice but to drop your expectations. (Okay, so this is my modus operandi!)

The kids' corner

Some homes have an entire room dedicated to the play area; others borrow a bit here and there, littering toys and craft in available corners and nooks. I once saw a playroom as big as my whole house, where my jaw dropped enviously at a wall-to-wall bespoke cabinet with pigeonhole-type storage for one family's plethora of games, toys and craft. But I'm similarly charmed when people work within smaller spaces and budget challenges.

What I've learnt from all my house-perving is that when there are children in the mix, what matters is not so much how much stuff you buy on their behalf, but the efficiency of your editing and recycling practices. Sure, buy them whatever you like, but don't let it hang around until they reach puberty. These toys and games can overtake your whole house unless you stay on top of them, and sometimes having limited space works wonders for keeping a tight rein on what comes in and goes out. Toy libraries are a godsend for modern parents (find listings at kidspot.com.au) but they're an underused resource. Not only do you get to borrow toys you'd never want to fork out for, you can get rid of large pieces of plastic when space is tight, which usually seems to coincide with the item in question losing its fascination for your child.

Sometimes all you need to keep things under control is a desk with storage that fits into a corner and an overhead shelf for holding jam jars full of stickers, pencils and crayons. Other times the Expedit bookcase from Ikea at $159 (ikea.com.au) is a satisfying hold-all. The general upkeep on either of these options is what makes them successful solutions. Ask yourself (don't trust your child to answer – we all know they have no real idea of time), 'When was the last time they played with that toy/game/instrument?' Two to three months is my cut-off, then it's out the door to St Vincent de Paul – unless, of course, it's one of their select, untouchable favourites.

Being a pathetic softie for anything my children ask for, I try to stick to a rule of buying one book for every crappy toy. From the bite-sized Mr Men paperbacks to hardback re-releases of the classics, the benefits of books are countless and truly long-lasting – not to mention they only take up a teeny amount of space. A space ratio of fifteen books to one toy? It's a no-brainer!

Here are seven books your children should read before they reach ten:

1. *Where the Wild Things Are* by Maurice Sendak
2. *The Magic Faraway Tree* by Enid Blyton
3. *Storm Boy* by Colin Thiele
4. *The Magic Pudding* by Norman Lindsay
5. *Little Women* by Louisa May Alcott
6. *The Lion, the Witch and the Wardrobe* by C. S. Lewis
7. *Alice's Adventures in Wonderland* by Lewis Carroll

The laundry as retreat

Phyllis Diller may be the most unlikely person from whom to take housekeeping tips, but her 'Cleaning the house while your kids are growing up is like shovelling the walk before it stops snowing' is gold. She's spot on – apart, of course, from the laundry.

Given the laundry is often the smallest room in the house, it could very well become the new retreat room. Why I like the laundry is that in spite of any other mess that's going on in the rest of the house, it's the easiest room to keep under control. And, along with bathrooms, laundries still haven't managed to lend themselves to multitasking. Not even if you tried! You can't really steal a kip in there, it's impossible to designate it a homework spot, and you can't house your laptop in there either.

Usually, laundries leave no space for design errors. And while some people are lucky enough to own a real, actual laundry (that is, a specific room, however small it might be, with a door on it) many others are forced to host a space-saving version in part of their bathroom, kitchen or a cupboard or nook. Sometimes it's not even a designated nook – I once had a laundry that was side by side with the tinned and dried goods in the pantry.

Apart from the more practical issues a laundry raises, I believe that a room dedicated just to the cleaning of clothes is a source of joy in itself. It would be far too presumptuous to give you tips on how to improve your own – as you well know, no two laundries are alike – but if you do ever have the chance to build one from scratch, please take the opportunity to consider water and space efficiency. Sun-dried laundry feels incredible, so if you have a backyard or a workable balcony you can possibly dispense with the dryer. And I would strongly recommend getting one of those gorgeously generous sinks in which French housewives do their flower-arranging. That way your laundry really will become a room to retreat to. Let's paraphrase George Herbert, who said it best, and make drudgery divine.

To render your laundry less depressing, dedicate a shelf to vases (keep them here rather than in the kitchen). Dressing flowers in the laundry tub really can make your day, and it transforms the laundry into a much more inviting room. Going there to do your flowers gives it a better energy than just going there to face the ongoing workload that is washing.

A cosy winter living room

In Europe it's not unusual to change the house when winter comes, and I don't mean just moving the chairs closer to the fireplace. They pull up the lighter weight rugs and replace them with toe-scrunching, heat-retaining versions. The breezier curtains are swapped for cold-repelling swathes. Some even invest in winter and summer cushions.

While our climate doesn't call for such drastic measures, it can be worthwhile thinking of your main living area as one that can wear a winter coat or a summer slip. I know one homeowner who uses the power of flowers to mark the seasons in her sitting room: velvety 'Queen of the Night' tulips come July and hydrangeas, frangipanis and gardenias in the New Year.

Some living rooms are naturally more suited to winter while others come alive in summer. Apart from the room's orientation, its colour schemes play an important role in its overall adaptability to winter or summer. I've found that the best two-timers are neutral rooms – they can take the dark chocolate colours in winter just as easily as ivories and hints of blue in the warmer months.

Here are four suggestions for the bare necessities to invest in for winter:

1. Rugs (of both the floor and lap variety!) – They can act like a warm hug when you come home. I'm a fan of the gimmicky lap rug with built-in electric-blanket device, which allows those sharing it their own mini climate control. For the floor, nothing is better than feel-good natural fibres. Sure, they can give the Dyson a workout, but just think of your feet.
2. A single chair – Somewhere to sit, relax and read. Sheepskin, leather and wood are ideal, as their inherent beauty is so much more apparent when they're part of a small single seat rather than a larger lounge suite.
3. A mug – Whether you prefer milky French lattes or a fireside sherry, a homely drinking vessel is a less expensive way to welcome the winter. The right kind of glass or mug can double as a bud vase in the summer anyway.
4. Cushions – They are as vital to a lounge as lipstick to the little black dress. They can add a necessary dose of glamour, fun, warmth or interest to the most boring of lounges. I like to think of cushions as a toe-dipping exercise – if you don't want to go the whole hog with a pinstripe two-seater, you can go there with a gorgeous oblong pinstripe cushion. It's here that you can play with detail and embellishment on a risk-free small scale.

Here are some tips for keep your heating bill down:

1. Retain heat from the daytime sun – Build your living room with north-facing windows to absorb the daytime sun then radiate the heat at night.
2. Exclude drafts around windows and under doors – Hang curtains and blinds with pelmets, use draft excluders and install double glazing.
3. Put insulation in the ceiling and walls – It truly makes a difference.
4. Install an energy-efficient heating system – Reverse-cycle air-conditioning can be quite efficient, but try turning it down one degree and you'll reduce your energy consumption by as much as fifteen per cent.

The elegant night-time living room

Some places are just meant to be devastatingly handsome at night. I know this for a fact, as I believe that I look my nicest come the p.m., too. I'm just puffy, rushed and a bit sad in the mornings, but by night-time I'm convinced that I'm my true self: more confident, smilier and generally more attractive. Sometimes I even have to go home at about three p.m. to shower and re-dress, so that I can feel completely that the morning didn't happen.

When I walk into rooms, I judge them to be either morning or night-time rooms. Some rooms are born for serving whisky sour, playing backgammon and reading Keats, while others are just waiting for eggs sunny side up and sunshine. This poses a problem when the room you envisage as your breakfast room has actually been put on this earth to be a night-time room. That's something only you, the owner of the home, can decide. A night-time room, I'd say, would more than likely have the worst orientation in the house. It would probably also be the smallest on the floor plan (apart from the toilet or laundry).

Here are my favourite night-time-room tricks:

- Dark paint – Eclipse by Covered In Paint (coveredinpaint.com.au) is a beautiful dark shale. Go wall to wall. Never have a feature wall. Ever.
- Candlelight – Could you get any cleaner or more natural than pure beeswax candles? The best I have come across are by Queen B (queenb.com.au) and Northern Light (northernlight.com.au).
- Things you love but that don't look so good in full-blown sunlit rooms – These may be some of those givens (see page 186) you have to keep because they're heirlooms or from your well-intentioned partner. Put them in this dark little special room and they'll magically blend in.
- A serious stereo system – The best thing about dark rooms is that you need only (or *I* think you need only) clean your dust-magnet hi-fi every other time.
- Put your television in here – As I detest televisions for their ability to wreck lovely sun-filled rooms, a night-time-room television, if the household lets you get away with it, is ideal.
- Choose a good feature piece – When something is placed in the light in a dark room, it's highlighted and extra noticeable.
- Go further than you usually would – The pieces you use to deck out this room won't bore you in the same the way as your other things you see more often. Go out on a limb with things for which you wouldn't usually have the gumption.

The perfect guest room

I know a couple who built a house with no internal doors, which means that their guests only ever end up staying for one night. At the other end of the spectrum, I know a hostess with the mostest who has made her guest room so outrageously comfortable that she has had to start a roster to keep track of all the bookings.

Creating the perfect guest room is a lovely and generous idea if you have spare space and a little time. When putting a guest room together, go about it in exactly the opposite way you would when thinking about your own bedroom. Because our main bedrooms are the rooms least likely to be seen by our guests, they tend to lack the charm or attention we lavish on the other rooms in the house.

What the guest room offers is the chance to turn a decorative trick: it's time to channel Four Seasons rather than Formule1. Gone are the constraints of a real working room that has to be in service seven days a week: this is your chance to show some real flair, consider something over the top or try something new. Think outlandish. Think ridiculous. Think soaps on pillows (rather than those predictable chocolates). Think fluffy towels reserved for stay-overs only. Think bedside tables with drawers for smalls. Think lamps that double as vases. Think sheets with fancy trimmings. Think candles you'd never dream of buying for yourself. The best thing about this kind of set-up is that once your guest goes, you can leave the room as it is – a trophy of sorts. It need not be touched or wrecked again until the next guest checks in. Beautiful unused space – heaven!

Another bonus to doing up a guest room is that it's a reminder: if you're providing a lovely haven for a weary head or a faraway friend now, then some day, somewhere in the world, someone might do the same for you.

Here is a guest-friendly tactic: spoil them with flowers and candles. I never used to believe in overpriced candles – until I discovered Cire Trudon's perfumed candles in brown glass (ciretrudon.com). I love that the candles burn for seventy hours and that you can then use the handsome hand-blown glass as a vase. Violets cut short look just incredible in these vessels. For more tips on flowers, see page 205.

Deck your hallway

I've always thought that the word 'hallway' falsely suggests roominess – the 'way' part has certain connotations of space. This long, often narrow void that runs through the centre of the house is usually its smallest space, but we expect it to accommodate the most mess. Used and abused as a communal dumping ground, it's no wonder the area gets a little wayward at times.

Our great expectations and its small dimensions make the hallway a difficult room to conquer, decoratively speaking. In my experience, most people never really decorate their hallways – furniture just seems to make its way there on the way out of or into the house. And given that the hallway is an area that everybody, even the dog, just passes through to get to more exciting rooms, there's a general feeling that it's not worth bothering to make it look more interesting. I guess the other key factor is, since lounges can cost as much as a small car, there's rarely any money left over to spend on a space that doesn't even count as a room.

Some inspired decorators attack hallways by introducing a feature piece – when there's enough space – but I take it as an opportunity to maximise storage. And I don't mean floor-to-ceiling cupboards or a huge Chinese wedding cabinet, but things that can do double duty for you – look good but still perform some function. Until recently, the options for hallway furnishings have been pretty task-specific, but thanks to the wave of space-hungry apartment-dwellers, there has been resurgence in pieces that are on the skinny side, do their best to look fabulous and tackle a task all at the same time. Coat hooks that look like moose heads, side tables that are trimmed and slim, key holders that deceptively look like framed pictures are all on offer, along with new takes on old classics.

If you *do* want to spruce up your hallway, it's the perfect place to try a feature wall, either at the very end or along both sides. I once styled a house that was doused in Resene's Brown Bramble (resene.com.au). It was like walking through a maze of chocolate – warm, decidedly decadent and a great front-of-house statement. I also think it's best to resist the urge to hang all your best artworks down the hallway – much better to give your best pieces a wider audience by placing them in rooms where people actually stop for a while.

If you take away just one idea for your hallway now, it should be this: splurge on a fabulous lamp. It's all the decoration a skinny area needs, will be the one memorable piece that doesn't take up useable space and is neither purely functional nor storage-related.

Hallways love lights, and lights really do have the power to transform a room. Here are the sites I love to visit:

- jfchen.com – An international beauty with immaculate vintage lights, among other things. You'll never see a duplicate here, and all their pieces are of collector standard. Big bucks territory!
- circalighting.com – An American light house like no other. I love all those preppie styles and creamy alabaster bases – magnificent shade-and-base combinations at every click!
- artemide.com.au – Drool, Italian-style, for modern looks only. Red hot!
- mondoluce.com. au – Great styles and some well-priced local beauties.

Working with and under a staircase

It's pretty simple with staircases: depending on how you value space you either build in a dark, endlessly deep storage cupboard or you use the space for the decorative good of the house. Instead of giving the camping gear and vacuum their very own hidey-hole, why not reveal rather than conceal the space? Beautiful book spines, objects and collectables can all have a home in a generous under-stair space. If your house has no natural sitting room, the hallway under the stairs – with the right chair – can make for a great impromptu getaway room. Once you put shelves in, no matter how big or small they are, it's amazing how quickly you'll find stuff (whether it's junk or desirables) to fill them up.

Those of you who want to cleverly borrow space from the under-stairs void should consider some of the following decorative options – you might not get away with them successfully in any other room:

1. An oversized painting – Stairwells are the prime spot to ensure all visitors as well as occupants of the house get to truly appreciate the work.
2. A comfy chair and a table top – You can turn this into a sneaky desk as long as you're vigilant about keeping reminders of daily life to a minimum or in a storage box or clever built-in drawer.
3. Bookshelf lighting – People light their swimming pools and backyards at night; a bookshelf is no different. When a lit bookshelf is positioned in the centre of the house, it makes for beautiful central lighting.
4. A bolt of colour – Feature walls can be tricky, especially if the wall is taken up by bookshelves, and sometimes they fail to feature anything but the wrong choice of colour. Placing a wall of colour under the stairs can be like saying to the world, 'See I *do* do colour,' even though the rest of the house is doused in neutrals.
5. Decorate your bookshelves with bookends – Novelty or pedigreed, they're a great way to style up a not-quite-full shelf of books.
6. Splurge on a floor covering – Rugs are the decorative element du jour. One in the right shape will make the under-stairs area seem more like a room.

Generally speaking, though, when it comes to under the stairs, it's best to stick to larger scale things. Small objects and frames will actually work against the space and come across all bitty – the staircase is the place for bigger, luscious brushstrokes.

The corner office

These days, home offices really do go way beyond small. Some have entire floors turned over to them, while others are, thanks to sexy wireless connections, the invisible office, the teeny-weeny office and even the bedside-table office.

This section should help you inch closer to the goal of being your own boss some day or of being the boss of a lot of other people remotely. Somewhere in between the kitchen, dining and living room, there's usually an unused corner that's near a power point – and that's really all you need. I've seen some snazzy home offices down hallways, in bedrooms, on side tables in living rooms and scooped out of kitchen niches.

Basically, any room can defy the floor plan and host a nook. Most design houses and furniture retailers recognise the importance of the home office, so we're spoilt for choice when it comes to desks that close themselves up. It's important to judge these most of all on their ease of use and storage capacity. You need something that has built-in room for pencils and stationery so you can avoid messy pen holders, and it needs to hide away the hard drive if that's the way your technology is set up.

Once you've found your corner and bought the desk, the staples you'll then need are:

- Desk lamp – I prefer an elbowed lamp that can be pulled in and out. The higher the lamp the better, so check that the lamp is taller than the computer screen it will illuminate.
- Chair – If your 'office' is not a true high-use work area, now is the time to splurge on a great hero chair, one you'd never, ever have more than one of. A feature chair can really have an impact in an otherwise ho-hum corner.
- Storage – Try to shop for a lidded inbox and outbox – you might not have the work under control, but at least the paper will be.
- Hold-alls – There are plenty of beautifully hued folders, journals and files on the market that will be both functional and beautiful home-office additions. If it's a shared family space, you could designate one colour per person, or stick lovely labels on one colour or print.
- Extras – While most computers have a built-in clock, a desk clock brings elegance to any office set-up. Also think about a dish for keys and change or even a hook or message board for household communications.

If you're lucky enough to work from home officially, don't ever complain. If you can make it work, you have the dream job!

The home office is the one area that threatens the home's green status. Select black-and-white as the default on your home printer and even consider printing in a typeface that takes up less ink (see ecofont.eu for a free, earth-saving download).

A room of one's own

It's an elusive concept – foreign to many, but still held dear – the idea that you could one day, when you become a grown-up, have a room all of your own. It's an enticing quest. This compact little me-room is the stuff decorative dreams are made of – unless, of course, your house is already brimming with spare rooms!

No matter what your residential status, it's a very worthwhile room to plan for in your head. I'm always thinking about the kind of room my own would be. I often wonder, for example, if I'd really paint all the walls in a soft colour and I toy with fabric swatches. It's the ultimate luxury to play decorator in the one room no one else ever uses. It's a place where all your favourite colours, things, bits and pieces can sit unharmed and unmolested. An iPod or radio is mandatory, so you get to have your own soundtrack, and the room (now we're really getting into wet-dream territory) should have a small hotel-like bar fridge containing your favourite sup. My room would also have lots of books, art hung in a French-hang style (see page 112), a telephone with my favourite people's numbers programmed in, milky-coloured ceramics, complete sets of my fave decor magazines and, of course, a window through which natural light pours in. It would also have geraniums, a stash of licorice and a super-cushy chair. Best of all, it would be too pokey to allow me to entertain any more than one visitor at a time.

When you actually think about the elements you'd have in your room, you get a step closer to it becoming a reality. A child moves out of home, a wall gets put up, a windfall comes through for a reno and, before you know it, it's well within your reach and happening. It's like your trademark room, answering to no one, servicing only you and your whims.

Men have sheds (or at least used to; see page 38), women have rooms, so it's time to dream up your own. While we're on the subject, there's an old book I love called *A Room of Her Own: Women's Personal Spaces* by an American author, Chris Casson Madden. It's very daggy compared with the racy reno books out at the moment, but it's into its ninth reprint. It reports (in both words and pictures – most satisfying) on the dreamy getaways of women from all walks of life. There's Ali MacGraw's yoga room, futurist Faith Popcorn's pad and the beautiful sleeping quarters of a nun in the New Mexican desert. Buy it – and many more hardbacks – to read in your own dream hideaway.

Here are the colours I'd pick if I had a room of my very own:

- Lilac – Specifically Resene Fog (resene.com.au).
- Powder blue – B at 1% from the Natural Paint Place (thenaturalpaintplace.com.au).
- Grey – 20/30 Bauwerk Über (bauwerk.com.au). It's truly beautiful!

A room of *his* own

Everyone should have a room of their own (see page 36), and sometimes, if you're lucky, your floor plan will allow it to happen. Men need their own room just as much as women do – somewhere to tinker, play, dream and contemplate. This would once have been the shed, but shrinking blocks and other impacts of modern life have made sheds almost extinct.

I'd love a room where I could leave things for my husband to fix – although they'd have to be things within his skill set. For now we have a cupboard for this: it's a 'to do' cupboard for both him and me. He leaves things in there that are within my achievable range and I for him. It's so chockers at the moment, we can't open if for fear of hurting the children. So the plan now is to save up and pay someone to come and spend a week tending to all the little fixes.

Many men, though, have their 'own' room. Some are breakaway areas in other rooms, bordered off by shelving, while others are full closed-door jobs. They all come under the guise of 'a desk away from the office', so yes, there *is* a computer hooked up. But if you look beyond that, it's really just a place where all their follies can live harmoniously – and there's nothing wrong with that.

Whenever I'm hunting for treasures, I try to find a place nearby where the boys can go. I have some great matches: in my favourite stomping ground, the Southern Highlands, there's Peppergreen Antiques in Berrima for girls (perfect for ribbons, quilts and kitchenalia) and then The Shed in nearby Mittagong for the boys (for farm machinery, car parts and sinks that need saving).

Some of the best places have been ones I've stumbled upon off the beaten track. They trade without flashy websites and usually don't even have a business card to offer, but they're the gems of our trips. I know that the fun comes in finding your own haunts, but here's a list of some really reliable places that are *not* off the beaten track:

- Doug Up On Bourke – 901 Bourke Street, Waterloo NSW 2017, (02) 9690 0962 (douguponbourke.com.au).
- Heritage Building Centre – Rear 432b West Botany Street, Rockdale NSW 2216, (02) 9567 1322 (heritagebuilding.com.au).
- The Junk Company – 583 Elizabeth Street, Melbourne Vic. 3000, (03) 9328 8121 (thejunkcompany.com.au).
- City Collectables Shop – 117 Elizabeth Street, Hobart Tas. 7000, (03) 6231 4838.
- Warwick Oakman – 62 Sandy Bay Road, Battery Point Tas. 7004, (03) 6224 9904.

Craft room nirvana

I have a friend who's just completed a rather spiffy renovation. It ticks all the boxes: it's pretty much picture-perfect, came in only a single digit above budget, works as a family house, and has made her husband, kids and cat happy. She recently confided, though, that while the house is indeed 'perfect', she's thinking of putting up a flyer in the local area looking for an unused garage or garret to rent. Since she can't handle real mess or a work in progress, she sees this rented room as a nirvana she and her daughters can escape to and play in without reservation, much like the attic room fathers and sons used to use for playing with trains. Her plan is for them all to paint, make long-term mess, plot projects, have mad fun times and do craft to their heart's content. Knowing her, she'll find something just right and it will be a wonderful getaway – restorative, creative and calming.

You might be one of those lucky people who already *has* the spare room for an onsite craft room. God bless your fortunate cotton socks – the key to a balanced life can be yours! Coming from a long line of crafters, my Holy Grail is a dedicated craft room, but in my current are-we-renovating/are-we-not, treading-water stage, I don't have a spare room I can dedicate to the purpose. It's high on my list of priorities, up there with the bathroom and kitchen, and I know it's the one room that will give me unsung pleasure. In the meantime, I have a scaled-down shelf in the linen cupboard to house the bare necessities.

Craft is possibly the wrong word, though – it implies non-Etsy-style needlework and scrapbooking, whereas it should perhaps be renamed the Frippery Room. I would put all my favourite bits of frippery: wrapping paper, interesting postcards, cards (buying them is a disease – I could go to thirty weddings, ten funerals and fifty housewarmings and still have cards left over), stamps, scissors, books and music. In one corner I might have seeds I have no intention of ever planting and in the other magazine tear sheets I have no plan ever to follow up on. There would also be a dumping ground for things to frame, and disks full of photographs to process. Use yours for wrapping presents, creating art with your kids, reading poetry, making models, collecting fabric scraps, whatever it might be.

One day I'll have a room just like this one. Imagine the indescribable joy that could come from this room – I could be so happy here! No tidying up, just mess-making. Sure, you don't ever see 'craft room' touted in the real-estate ads, but that's just the point – if you had one of these, you'd probably find it hard to leave.

I love the scissors-and-string unit from heaveninearth.com.au. Any room can benefit from its humble usefulness, and even men will appreciate its dual-purpose ingenuity.

The rooftop conversion

There's not much incentive to move these days. Given the cost involved (emotional as well as financial), I'm surprised that more homeowners looking to upgrade don't consider the roof-conversion option. It can, in one fell swoop, transform an average three-bedder into a four-bedroom mansion – a significant leap in real-estate terms – and secure superior district, seaside or city views without taking up more land. A designer friend of mine, Sally McBean, recently converted unused space in her terrace roof into an amazing spare room. Her son couldn't be happier with his new play-den at the top of the stairs, nor could visiting relatives, who now have a dedicated room in which to stay or family members just wanting to escape the everyday bustle of the lower floors.

Of course, most homeowners go into their roof to create real bedrooms and living spaces rather than play- or spare rooms. It's potentially a massively valuable commodity in high-density urban enclaves. McBean, for instance, was able to squeeze another 90 square metres from an area that previously hadn't even offered any storage.

If you're moving into your roof, keep the following in mind come fit-out time:

- Build a proper staircase – The pull-down variety is annoyingly makeshift and reminiscent of something you'd see on an aircraft. (But expect to lose a minimum of 3 metres of floor space in order to create said staircase.) If it's only a storage room, though, those unsightly (but – okay, okay – nevertheless nifty) pull-down attic ladders can cost about $500, still a lot cheaper than a built-in wardrobe.
- Give your new room a specific purpose – Music room, library or TV room, for example. Or it could be a girls' own space, like the room in this photograph.
- Get your structural engineer to outline load-bearing capacities before you drag up all your heavy boxes of books – Older-style houses are usually better equipped in this regard, given they have hardwood joists, which are typically stronger than more modern but flimsier treated-pine joists. Each square metre needs to be able to bear up to 400 kilograms of weight.

Study, darkroom, den, chess room or craft room: squeezing attic space out of a roof is the way to accommodate a specialist hobby. Heaven of all heavens would be a magazine room! Imagine wall-to-wall magazines and a reading chair – now that's worth climbing the stairs for. If you love magazines and find yourself in Melbourne, make a visit to Mag Nation – that's right, a shop devoted just to magazines of every kind. Of course they have a great design and interiors section. Find them at 88 Elizabeth St in the city, 110–112 Greville St in Prahran or magnation. com.

The outdoor getaway

Making your own getaway might be easier than you think. Here are some stunningly obvious and not-so-obvious ideas and tips for creating outdoor spaces – after all, it really can add another 'room' to your floor plan, sans any gruelling, hard-yards renovation:

- Seats – There's nothing more high-maintenance and boring than rushing out at the slightest drop of rain to bring in cushions and daybed coverings. Seville Seaside is a gloriously blue-based skinny-stripe option from weatherproof-fabric experts Sunbrella (sunbrella.com) – fab for banquette seating or daybeds.
- Music – Exterior speakers can really bring the backyard to life, and you can go for snazzy-looking cube speakers, or speakers camouflaged as rocks or waterproof balls (see lenwallisaudio.com.au).
- Hammock – I've found a fabulous beauty at hammockstore.com.au. It has boho styling (think Jade Jagger poolside at her Ibiza residence), long fringed crocheted sides and is available in glorious tangerine.
- Tubtrugs – Get some for leaf-collecting, rose-chilling, puppy-washing, pool-toy-storing, pet-accessory collation. I like the large, shallow 35 litre one in vanilla or grey. Possibly the best twenty-odd dollars you'll ever spend.
- Outdoor furniture – Check out the pretty faux bamboo options in the Alboo range at robertplumb.com.au. The Foxy three-seater (with white frame option) is fabulous and can be left outside, rain, hail or shine.
- Paving – I love pavers, but hate the defeated concrete-jungle look. Growing herbs in between can make the cheapest pavers look decidedly Euro. Adbri make a great 40 × 40 centimetre paver called Euro Classic (cmbrick.com.au). Have them laid with 2 centimetre gaps between them and plant the embarrassingly easy-to-grow creeping woolly thyme there.
- Trees – Tall trees have so much more visual impact than anything in a low flowerbed. Gardening is a bit like money – it's easy to make excuses like, 'Gee, if only I had more money/space, I'd be a much better saver/gardener.' I've had plots both large and indecently small, and I've been a hopeless green finger in both. But trust me, anyone can buy their very own Japanese weeping maple at the Winter Hill Tree Farm (winterhill.com.au). It can live potted, in part or full sun if its soil is kept moist. So imagine, then, if you had three, spaced them a little, hung pretty festooning lights between them and dined beneath their canopy. You'd have the best seat in the house!

Warehouse living

Warehouse living basically requires more of everything – more artwork, more tables, more places to sit, more shelving and more insulation. It's difficult to deck out a warehouse, but it's a highly rewarding and extremely sexy way to live. Make grand statements and big gestures, and ensure you have adequate heating and cooling. Try these tips:

- Lay out the length of your dining table on the warehouse floor (try newspaper cut to size) – Even the biggest twelve-seater can come across a little flaky in a large space. Some warehouse-dwellers push two eight-seaters together.
- Your dining chairs should be fairly consistent – Don't practise random-chair cuteness: strike boldly.
- Build in or bring in as much storage as possible – You and your budget will need to be prepared to go the extra mile for large-scale and seemingly bulky units.
- Use storage units, shelving systems and cupboards as room dividers – Make cosier segments within the one expanse, adding privacy, increasing the sense of room division and creating warmth.
- Consider using the vertical space – I saw a fab loft warehouse (home to three kids) with a drop-down swing, placed so the swinger never encountered a wall!
- For cooling, consider overhead fans rather than air-conditioning units – Fans allow you to cool only those areas of the house you need to, and they're aesthetically more warehouse-friendly than a bulky air-con unit.
- Look for large artwork or be sure you have enough smaller to mid-sized pieces to fill a wall – Use the negative space to create beautiful voids between the works, putting the generous wall space to use. It's a good idea to hang the work slightly lower than in a normal house, to create a room-like intimacy.
- Invest in curtains of the billowing, sheer kind – They're the easiest way to soften the industrial edges of a warehouse space. An S-track hanging system rather than a curtain rod is a must in this situation.
- Expect to require custom solutions – Most rugs won't cover the floor space adequately, so price a piece cut and edged to size. Rugs divide up the floor space.
- Don't go mad on oversized mirrors – Unless you're adding some strategic light in a dark area. Mirrors multiply everything, making it all look even smaller.
- Consider the Link sideboard (2.49 × 0.54 × 0.66 metres) from Poliform (poliform.com.au) and the Apartamento Cardboard Stool from Design for Use (designforuse.com.au).

keeping up
appearances

The *new* new romantic

Is it old or is it new? Is it a little bit country or a tad rock'n'roll? The new romantic is a delightful hybrid of the two. It takes the best from the old and mixes it with the new to make both a little better. It's not as frothy and frilly as last season and, thankfully, it goes a little softer on the floral intake. It's casual and fresh all at once, and can easily update a tired French-provincial or shabby-chic space.

What makes this decorating trend so adorable is taking some of the more comforting aspects of the late eighteenth century and intermixing them with more modern items. Painted furniture and pieces that look like they've been brought in from the garden all work to ensure that the informal look is kept, well, unkept. And instead of the complete flower explosion of the style's previous incarnation, we now have a slightly weathered posy.

The best part about the trend? Your rooms don't have to be pin-tidy: its looseness lets your sitting rooms, dining nooks and living spaces stay in a lived-in state. And while there are no hard-and-fast rules, here are some take-them-if-you-care-to guidelines:

- Go for a predominately neutral base – It will help make the other tonal and floral elements work harder.
- Add a hard piece of furniture (in metal or wood) – Use it to display all your soft and cushy pieces.
- Use greens and soft blues – Choose them over the usual pinks and sorbet colours.
- Make white your friend – Use it on the floors and walls, and in soft furnishings.
- Display pretty-hued glassware and everyday porcelain.
- Offer ample seating – It's all about comfort.
- Return to curtains – They're so much softer than blinds and shutters.
- Consider industrial lighting – It's a great light source and really adds character as a one-off.
- Use the street or your garden as your flower source rather than the florist – This will give you random, naturally beautiful arrangements. You can even put the kitchen garden and herbs to work in small jugs and vases.

This is a look that allows you to defy price and provenance, and to intermix high-street buys with antiques and charity-store finds with investment pieces.

A splash of floral can be charming and you won't need a lot to add to the magic. I dream of a padded screen in a vintage Sanderson cotton. Here are some fabric showrooms that have a great range of modern florals, and while you'll probably need a designer or decorator to buy on your behalf, they're at the very least an inspiring starting point. Discover printed blooms you've never seen before at Mokum (mokumtextiles.com), Zepel Fabrics (zepelfabrics.com.au) and Warwick Fabrics (warwick.com.au). If you still haven't found what you're after, try fabric sales, remnant traders and bric-a-brac sellers. I've found cheap second-hand florals, cleaned them up and sewn them into one-off cushions, accessories and soft covers.

How to be thoroughly modern

The thing about truly modern interiors is that most people all too quickly write them off as label-chasers or just plain lazy. 'Why would anyone deliberately choose to live among only a few key pieces?' they ask. The answer is pure and simple: modernism is both progressive and optimistic and is all about the good, the beautiful and the technically innovative. Modernist designers typically rejected unnecessary decorative motifs and preferred to let the materials and geometrical forms speak for themselves. So if open-plan interiors and the absence of clutter sound like home-heaven to you, maybe you're more of a modernist than you think.

Far from austere, elegant modernist spaces make a feature of extreme clarity and simplicity. The pioneers of this movement were Ludwig Mies van der Rohe (whose Seagram Building in New York City became the archetypal modernist building), Walter Gropius, Le Corbusier (he was born Charles Édouard Jeanneret but, like Madonna, got so famous he could get away with one name) and Lilly Reich. These clean-line-loving folk were reacting to the over-the-top, embellished ornamentation of the late nineteenth century and ensured that the departure was a dramatic one. Gilded wood and indulgent fabric gave way to the glitteringly simplicity of perfect polished metal. Visually heavy furniture returned to visually light, and suddenly clarity over clutter made sense.

The truly modern decorator is usually aiming for the ultimate in form meeting function and knows all too well that less can really be more. Practise being a modernist with these tips:

- Have a single-minded focus on such materials as glass and steel.
- Invest in iconic chairs – Single seats are the calling card of any decent modernist. Mies van der Rohe, well aware of the endless possibilities and problems with chairs, said it's 'almost easier to build a skyscraper than a chair'. Buy up! They're cheaper than skyscrapers.
- Crave spatial drama – Truly appreciate the uncluttered bliss that a void can create.
- Don't drool wishfully over curtain ads – Modernist window treatments are usually bare and clean.
- Have an understanding and appreciation of the influences on modernism, such as Bauhaus and Art Nouveau. True modernists keep a lot of weighty and expensive books on the subject close at hand.

Like any other decorating genre, modernism is best used in combination with other decorating styles – although purists would disapprove, knowing that God is in the details.

Becoming a modernist is sentencing yourself to a lifetime of cleaning, so you'll really need to know how to keep your glass table spotless. We all used to know that newspaper, water and elbow grease were best, but apparently newspapers aren't printed on the same kind of paper with the same kinds of inks any more. These days, in fact, it might leave you with dirtier glass than before! The best method is to spray the glass with a mixture of a little vinegar in water, then wipe in circular motions with paper towel until the glass is sparkling – pure and simple elbow grease.

Creating open-plan

Open-plan is not just for neat freaks. It's perfect for people who prefer quality to quantity or like to have it all out on show. It takes a certain confidence to pull it off, but the decorative courage of open-plan dwellers is rewarded with a wide space that's usually on the tidy side. What they lack in cosy quarters, they make up for in surround-sound systems, super-long tables to seat twelve and lounge rooms that twist and turn like road maps.

When you're dealing with a one-room, many-functions scenario, it's a never-ending challenge to strike a balance between a sense of space *and* a sense of enclosure. This is usually achieved by taking the room's decorative elements from similar genres. Whether you're going for handsome bachelor pad, parlour-style or a more earthy look, such stylistic consistency will cheat the space, making it appear larger than it is. If, for example, you have a magnificent chair and matching ottoman, it's best to honour the rest of the space with furniture and pieces of the same pedigree, but the open-plan room cannot simultaneously handle the top end and low end with the same kindness that other rooms can. Use light, colour and texture to create harmony within the whole space.

Try carving out flexible zones within the whole – one for each function. Take inspiration from hotel lobbies and public meeting spots: they incorporate smaller areas for relaxing, conversing and dining yet function as an attractive, seamless expanse. A light-coloured paint on walls and ceiling will make them visually recede, so that the room appears to be more spacious. Rugs can also help define each subsection, subtly suggesting rooms within a room, while floor left bare will denote thoroughfares. In smaller rooms you can afford to make a focal point of an artwork, an oversized object or a feature wall, but it's best to avoid this in a larger, open-plan room, where it can become a look-at-me punctuation mark.

It's wise to pay your cabinetmaker or joiner as much as you can afford to build in plenty of storage. Open-plan people get to consider impressively oversized lighting, artful rugs and coffee tables that are wide as well as deep and high. And a screen can work wonders. Used as a mess-hider or simply as a way to subdivide the room, it can be moved around to any corner.

When I lived open-plan I always thought I had more space than I did and my place became a magnet for things of ginormous proportions. The problem is, most open-plan rooms still have only standard-sized doorways. I can't tell you the pain of having to cut down the legs of my new lounge so it would fit through the door. Looks can really be deceiving, especially when it comes to open-plan.

With open-plan, it's best not to place all the furniture against the walls as you are usually forced to in a normal-sized room. Use their large shapes to break up the room – so make sure you buy a lounge chair that looks good from all angles. If you have too much Ikea (not a crime, just a suggestion) Aero Designs (aerodesigns.com.au) do nifty open-shelf cube systems that can act as room dividers.

Taking inspiration from nature

Mother Nature as an influence is a bottomless resource – she just gives and gives and gives. Buildings have been inspired by the shape of a leaf, paint colours have mimicked the colour of the head of a wave and countless room schemes have been based around the rich hues of a forest. But don't for a minute think that she's reserved for the left-brainers of this world. An American inventor was so taken with a group of mussels clinging to rocks, which he spotted while fishing, that he created a new adhesive for the building industry based on the molecular properties of the mussels' natural glue.

Back in the land of home worship, designers this season have taken direct inspiration from Mother Nature's many guises. Never have I seen so many beautiful botanical references in wallpapers, fabrics, lampshades, soft furnishings and table-top accessories. Her imprint is everywhere, both in the latest shapes and in the latest materials, such as water hyacinth, birch twigs, bamboo and linen. Perfect timing, too, I say – let's hope they serve as a constant reminder of what we have to lose by not caring enough for the real thing.

What I love most about studying nature is the incredible (not to mention free-of-charge) advice she willingly gives for paint schemes. Whether you're after that all-elusive neutral grey shell colour (try Murobond's Crushed Shell, murobond.com.au – it's exactly that), a shimmery soft brown similar to the trunk of a birch tree (try Porter's Elegance, porterspaints.com.au) or the colour of a storm (try Resene's Warlord, resene.com.au), I guarantee that any full colour scheme derived from nature will always be spot on. I've seen a cheery kitchen scheme based around the colours witnessed at an open-air fruit-and-veg market. I've styled a bathroom that took the incredible subtleties of a pebble as its muse and a master bedroom that took its cues from the super-soft colours of sea foam – a little each of grey, green and white-washed blue.

My favourite way to spot a winning combination is to look through my florist's window – there are hundreds of micro colour combos at work in every corner of the glass! Who knew that a single magnolia could hold all the secrets to painting a sitting room?

Shop up on nature from the following design houses:

- Cloth Fabric (clothfabric.com) – For a lamp made with beautiful textiles inspired by the Australian bush.
- KIFKAF (kifkaf.com.au) – For always-useful seagrass barrel baskets.
- Artemide (artemide.com.au) – For a wooden Danese Milano perpetual calendar you'll have forever and always.

Soft industrial

Industrial is one of those decor genres with many siblings – there's hardcore industrial and then the watered-down versions, hybrids intermixed with other trends to make them distinctively different yet familiar. What I love about working with industrial pieces is their commanding strength in a room, perfect for making a focal point or feature.

The industrial/found-furniture movement boomed when warehouse living was hot. High ceilings, exposed rafters, handsome worn dark floorboards and large windows were a perfect match for pieces with history. But then it all started looking, well, a bit samey. Just like a Victorian house with period furniture or a deco apartment with wall-to-wall 1940s furniture, industrial pieces in industrial spaces can look very hardcore and even dull. As designer Greg Natale attests, 'The interesting looks are always achieved when you mix it up.' French with minimalism, modern with baroque, contemporary with antiques: if done successfully, the polar differences in these combinations add a whole new level of interest to the room.

So when industrial-style pieces are placed in a white-on-white modern room, beautiful things can happen. In this photograph, the rarity of the old is matched by the beauty of the new, each making the other all the better for it. Magically, the room appears to be huge (white on white will always increase the perceived size of a room) and suddenly all the larger pieces seem to have some breathing room.

White is the perfect foil for interesting collections and objects – it lets you really show off aged pieces, and anything with a timeworn patina will command a sense of reverence when placed against white. Older pieces can now sit side by side with more luxurious pieces (just imagine how delicious a cashmere throw would be against aged wood), but the most fabulous thing about soft industrial is that it can always be worked up and improved upon – you never know when another fabulous forgotten thing will be hiding around the corner in a crazy store or market, whispering, 'Take me home. I'll make you happy forever.'

Old with new. Soft with hard. Here are some superb pairings:

- Stainless Steel four-poster bed from Pad Designer Furniture (pad.com.au) with a vintage Bakelite clock from davidmetnicole (davidmetnicole.com).
- Barbat + Suhr cashmere throw from Ondene (ondene.com.au) with a Globite suitcase from Doug Up On Bourke (douguponbourke.com.au).
- Tolix stool from Thonet (thonet.com.au) with a vintage light-bulb cage from davidmetnicole (www.davidmetnicole.com).

Australian rustic

Sick of designers dictating what your dining room should look like? Want to stop choreographing your clutter? Hark back to a simpler life? Look for a more natural way to live? Americans have the Shaker movement, we have rusticity. Who needs those divine French fresh cedar candles when your roof smells that good anyway? And what use is a fully loaded iPod when the rain is beating its own beautiful music on your corrugated roof? The times are changing, not just because designers are chasing eco-friendly materials but because modernity has come full circle. After excess, restraint usually follows.

Living rustically has long been the domain of true bush-dwellers or of weekenders who want to experience the opposite of their city lives after the working week. If you've ever hugged a tree and felt a zingy after-effect, then living among nature's offerings can have a similar but longer term impact. Real rustic, though, is not something you can actually buy – it involves a slow hunter–gatherer process of finding and combining special objects. I like it because it makes us question how many of our possessions we really do need and think about where they've come from.

Many among the design fraternity choose to live on the edge, surrounded by the elements. It's not hard to see why rusticity appeals to people whose day job is largely about what is manufactured. Architects are famous for it, spending as much time as they can living with the ultimate muse – nature. And not just architects. Sean Moran from Sean's Panaroma restaurant in Sydney lives in the thick of it for the working week but retreats to his mountain home on weekends, where he and his partner do all their 'living'. Russel Koskela and Sasha Titchkovsky from design firm Koskela do the same in a house they call Dickebusch, in a sleepy beach suburb surrounded by national park. Russel suggests that if you're finding it hard to get close to nature in your everyday home, then seeking out craftspeople who work with natural materials is an honourable way to start.

You can book your own rustic weekend away in Dickebusch through koskela.com.au. Find out just how beautiful it is to live among wood, wicker and fresh sea air.

A touch of luxury

We've recently been subjected to an influx of 'luxe' (be it über-luxe, plain old luxury or luxxxe), so it's probably a good time to take stock of what makes true luxury. For some it's cashmere cushions, hallmarked silver and throws made from the chin hair of endangered Peruvian animals. For others it can be living among furniture made only from Norwegian wood. For still others it's living only with what they need.

One sure way to achieve the whiff of luxury is with grey, pewter and silver. Individually elegant, when these tones are combined they can really lift a room to devastatingly luxurious heights, achieving an ambience in which men and woman can happily coexist without fear of being overly fluffed. With the addition of glass, crystal, mirrors and lead, things can really get dazzling.

Here are some tips from the top on how to create luxury in your home:

- Use grey as you would white – Go for it enthusiastically rather than restrict it to smaller feature walls, otherwise you'll risk creating a 'graphic' look rather than a soft and subdued one. Greys are also good for smaller spaces. Why try to make a small room look larger when you can celebrate its intimate proportions and maximise its cosy factor with a good dose of the greys?
- Spend up big on the smaller components – Select them in richer materials, such as cut crystal, mercury glass and silver to bring an element of unstudied formality.
- To add interest, select metallic pieces that have (or seem to have) an inherent age or patina.
- Counterbalance all the glass and metallics with a dose of softness – Choose welcoming window dressings, longer piled carpet and lots of throws and textures.

French designer Andrée Putman is the undisputed queen of luxury and, although she'd never let the word pass her Helena-Rubinsteined lips, she personifies it. It's in her every decorative action, but it's not her throws and glassware that add the real luxurious touch – it's the tones, surfaces and materials she employs in the room's initial build-up, which, when combined with the lighter pieces, look a zillion bucks. While Andrée's design fees restrict her services to hoteliers, trustafarians and developers, her quality-over-quantity mantra can be applied by us all.

If you had to spend your last decorating dollar in the name of luxury? Invest in a beautiful blanket or throw in a magnificent texture. It will warm up any room, adding another layer through its sheer existence. Blankets are basically teddy bears for grown-ups.

See some of Andrée Putnam's understated work in Hong Kong at the Putman (theputman.com). It has style in spades and lots of simple ideas that will inspire apartment-owners. She won't mind you copying – she's the Queen Bee!

Going for baroque

If objects could speak (I'm convinced they do), this room would say a great deal about its owners. When it comes to decorating, I'm constantly pulling myself back from overdoing it – but I revel in the glory when someone else has the guts to go all the way and then some. In spite of my own cowardice, I believe that overdone interiors can work as well as the beautiful, artfully empty ones – following the advice that good design is always on a tightrope of bad taste. In my styling travels I've seen many houses that go for it, but most magazines are reluctant to publish the pictures because they're out of line with the super-clean showroom look of the moment.

What I love about interiors that push the boundaries is that they allow you to blend traditional tricks in new ways. Lucite and brushed steel have had their moment of glory – now the time feels right for a genuine richness in both fabric and wallpaper. While it can never replace the all-important artworks, what wall decoration can do to a dining room goes beyond the effect of a painting.

There's a long tradition of artists collaborating on textiles – following in William Morris's footsteps, Dufy worked on the most wonderful fabrics, as did the Surrealists and many of the Bauhaus artists. It's just imagery on a larger scale. Major wallpaper and fabric houses are enjoying a resurgence of their more traditional patterns, but new printing businesses dedicated to producing bespoke designs have sprung up too. The most impressive I have seen, though, is Surface View (surfaceview.co.uk), which allows you to turn images from the V & A Museum archives into wall decoration. I have one of a large Japanese peony on its way as I write – I can't wait to hang it and let it take over the entire room.

The rooms that I think work best when overdressed are those you're not exposed to all the time – my peony will go in a sitting room where there's not much else to offer. I'm splurging on the peony and saving on the decoration, but I figure the room will be the better for it. Dining rooms (especially separate, formal ones), bathrooms, powder rooms and libraries are the perfect places in which to practise excess. Every time you enter, it's a real ooh-ahh moment. When your walls are full from floor to ceiling, you can get away with more courageous furniture: it becomes slightly camouflaged.

But, here is a tip re those wide-mouthed dining-table vases. The market, as you would know, is flooded with cheap ones of all sizes, but it's really a false economy to buy them when you consider how many flowers it takes to fill their super-wide mouths. I'd take a smaller, high-quality one any day. In the words of Angela Thirkell, one of my favourite writers, 'Never economise on luxuries.' So true.

For more on wallpaper, see 'Wallpaper redux' on page 114.

Bespeak your own wallpaper at Aficionados of the Nod (aficionados.com.au), Karman Grech Designs (kgdesigns.com.au), Publisher Textiles (publishertextiles.com.au) or Signature Prints (signatureprints.com.au). These companies apply a 'can do' attitude to even the smallest of print runs.

Bohemian rhapsody

Oh, thank you, glorious boho, for coming into our lives! You work as well in small rented bedrooms as you do in larger, overcapitalised spaces. Best of all, you have no hard-and-fast rules, no real right or wrong: just having a go is sometimes enough.

Bohemian style offers a relaxed, ad hoc look that complements the lifestyles of travellers and collectors, granting them the freedom to buy up wherever and whenever they will. (We *are* talking, after all, about the knack of artful clutter!) And it's certainly a relief for those who've never felt quite at home amid the clean, cool, uncompromising statements of minimalism. Boho can be feminine without being scarily over-the-top pretty and can never be anything other than brimming with personality. I've seen it work successfully in living rooms, bedrooms and bathrooms – but it is a particular boon to smaller rooms, where the gradual build-up of decorative elements has maximum impact.

And it is, of course, seductively low maintenance. Boho positively demands that your linen be slightly crumpled, your cushions mismatched, your bookshelves higgledy-piggledy and your bedside table, well, supporting a variety of objects. While it's true to say that this style could never turn its back on any colour, the ice-cream hues of raspberry, strawberry, orange blossom, spearmint, lemon, vanilla, latte and chocolate are shown to particular advantage in a boho setting.

Thanks to its affection for older style or revamped furniture, boho is also a relatively cost-effective aesthetic, especially if you can scour markets and second-hand stores for the major elements. What you save on the vintage bed head, for example, you can spend on the embroidered coverlet. One thing you must add to the splurge list is good candles: fragrant air and bohemia go hand in hand.

Paris Hotel Boutique (parishotelboutique.com) is an online store selling the contents of old French hotels (think plates, fur, hooks, cutlery and impeccable vintage books). There's no better way to start your French boudoir setting. On the exxy side but the real deal. Locally, Fleur Wood stores (fleurwood.com) offer lots in the way of satin bed accessories, sweetie-pie ornamentation and pieces with charm.

Charming the pants off a room

These days it's usual for the high-fashion mags to dedicate a few pages to a 'lifestyle' section, while the home and lifestyle mags dabble in a bit of light fashion. But there's a trend working its way through some of my favourite overseas decorating mags – they take a top-end fashion look and make it into a 'room'. I've seen a successful room version of Ms Audrey Hepburn – boho and tartan – and I have the tear sheets to prove it. The more likely applications are Ralph Lauren as a classic living room whose charms would never expire, Jil Sander as the ultimate pared-down, restful bedroom and Matthew Williamson as a dining room for hosting the most wonderful dinner parties.

The outfit-as-a-room makes for satisfying magazine fodder, but it's a hard one to live with out here in the real world. I think most people, unless they're truly wedded to one style, want a room that's the complete opposite of a prescribed outfit. My guess is that what we secretly want is our own little sitting room – much like our favourite jumper, scarf or hat (you know, the one you can't ever bear to throw away) rather than a designer pantsuit. Slightly time-worn, a tad unpredictable and completely and utterly comfortable – a happy accident of stripes, flowers and prints that, when put together, improve on each other. How glorious!

That said, perhaps the best way to start adding your own personal charm to a room is to look to your wardrobe and how you dress – not for a complete interpretation, but more for a little kick-start. Treat it like a basic lesson in what styles you naturally steer towards. Sure, it won't nail the room, but it could very well give you an idea for a lounge and cushion option you would never have considered before or help you find a texture or tone that wasn't even on your radar.

On the flipside, next time you're in a fashion fix, turn the tables and take a lead from your sitting room. As I can only give all my love and attention to one discipline – and that's all things home – when it comes to fashion I'm out of my depth, but I would definitely kill for the chance to wear an outfit that was this room. Floral, jewels, linen, embroidery and piped edges, all with a neutral undertone? Pure charm!

Fashion and homewares are explicitly linked. Fashion giant H&M (hm.com) are now offering an affordable range of bed linen and tableware. My other favourite fashion and homewares retailer is Anthropologie (anthropologie.com) in the USA. Neither ships to Australia, but make a beeline for them when you're next overseas. See 'Resources' on page 209 for more inspiring home-loving shops to visit when you're next in Paris, London, New York, Milan or Tokyo.

Achieving modern architectural

Austere minimalism (which now appears as ridiculous as the ornamental clutter emblematic of the Rothschilds' aesthetic) has made way for a beautiful middle ground. Somewhere between overstuffed and pared down lies modern architectural. More and more Australians are employing architects to build their dream houses, a clear indication that we're becoming increasingly aware of the impact of our immediate built environment and of our ability to control it. One of the benefits of this general awareness is that Australians are choosing to live within beautiful buildings rather than buying up on 'things' to make an ugly house beautiful.

Not every budget stretches to the attention of an architect, and not every job requires the skills of one, but I have noticed a few things in my house-perving profession that are worth passing on:

- Architects can be worth every cent and then some. After all, they've studied full time for seven years just to understand how to manipulate sunshine and space!
- Good design and architecture can be like music for the eyes.
- If there's a view, a vantage point, a focal point, or simply a pleasant outlook, an architect will dutifully (and rightly) frame it.
- When building new or renovating, consider the house or room's overall sustainability.
- Reduction is a recipe worth practising – ask yourself if there's an easier way to achieve the look you're after.
- Fussy window dressings can help disguise a room, but going brave and bare celebrates the space and offers the view of both inside and out.
- Don't fill your space for the purpose of filling it – in some situations, voids can speak louder.

The late decorator Billy Baldwin once said, 'I've always believed that architecture is more important than decoration. Scale and proportion give everlasting satisfaction that cannot be achieved by only icing the cake.' So when in doubt, throw stuff out. Or better still, just don't buy it in the first place. Invest, instead, in everlasting design. He also said, 'Nothing at all is better than second-best. Never fill an empty space just to fill it. Second-best is expensive, while nothing costs nothing.' Oh, so true!

Visualising your dream home

On my shelf, along with the family albums, my all-time favourite books and mandatory keepsakes, is an unnamed folder. It's big, it's bulging and it holds tear sheets of interiors that I will have one day when I grow up. They're different from the things I lust after today – the kinds of things I'm filing away for my future prosperity are elegant lounges filled with feathers and down (rather than a comfortable polyester mix), side tables whose only job is to display (rather than be overburdened) and tables of heirloom quality (not just make-goods). I dream of investment pieces that will go on to last a lifetime and I imagine them in a serene space where we all just flit about. In real life, though, we have to negotiate a litter of toys, chairs awaiting upholstery and must-do washing pile-ups.

Creative visualisation is the key to achieving much in life. Most psychologists employ it as means of turning inspiration into reality, and I recommend it wholeheartedly for dressing a room and playing house. It's really what interior decorators and designers are doing when they use a mood board. The professional ones show the suggested elements within the proposed room along with some mood-inducing shots, but it's really just a tool they use to communicate an overall idea.

You don't need a designer or decorator to do it for you, though. A shoebox filing 'system' can do the same thing, as can a renovation file or a 'When I grow up' folder. Keeping images of a space or room (even if its budget and size are vastly different from your own) is the key. A paint chip along with a tile along with an inspiring shot could be all the clues you need to create your next bathroom. This system is a practical one, but it can also act as a general thought-starter for everyone involved in the renovation process – they won't all have visualised as you do.

I hang on for dear life to a Polaroid of a room that was doused in blues and green as the perfect rebuttal to the old adage that 'Blue and green should not be seen without a colour in between'. Use your own file to express what you want from your decorator, cabinetmaker, painter or partner.

Arent&Pyke (a young and up-and-coming design firm) have just finished making over a fabulous family home – a real pager-turner in magazine terms. The budget was reasonable, the stock came in on time, and the clients are ecstatic, but the designer girls attribute their success to the fact that the owner (a working mother) apologetically handed over a cake box filled with miscellaneous pieces, saying that a written brief would follow. Once they'd gone through the things she'd collected, it was crystal clear to them what she wanted – no written brief could have done that. It really is true that a picture can paint a thousand words.

Design blogs are great for inspiration and you can show your favourites to design professionals in the knowledge that they speak the same language. My favourite is remodelista. com, because it covers hard-to-source and hard-to-explain fittings, and both hard and soft materials. If you'd like to see my own design work, please skip over to HOME's site, makingbeautiful. com.au, check out our gallery and sign up for our newsletter. For more blog ideas, see page 92.

It's all in the mix

While some people find reassurance in kitting out their spaces top to tail in designer furniture, others know all too well that there's cleverness and ingenuity in a mix. And you can apply this rule to pretty much everything. The well-dressed woman who puts together designer, vintage and mainstream pieces can come off looking more interesting than her completely Gucci-clad counterpart. But as you may also know, some people find solace in the one genre, knowing that if they buy it all it's a guaranteed good look.

There can be real beauty in mixing interiors, and the results are unpredictable and exciting. Whether it's old meets new, east meets west or top shelf meets lower end, it's all in the mix. Some people are born great mixers – you know those people who can just fling a thing here, a piece there, add another, often random element and it just looks outrageously good. Others work at it until they achieve a mix they're comfortable with, knowing that they can tone it down or ramp it up if their mood changes or the need arises. Still others hone their mixing abilities through a genuine interest in the world and an untamed eye (and wallet) when it comes to travelling. And some simply don't like being told how to dress their spaces from a catalogue or a 'lookbook'.

Mixing is something *everyone* can try, no matter what their decorating experience or taste. Some of the best mixers I know have achieved their skill through the best teacher of all – budgetary constraints. 'Save versus splurge' is a theory that has served me well, through both good times and bad. Adhere the best you can to a set budget, find the key pieces you need to buy no matter what their asking price, then pick up the rest using savvier shopping methods, such as sales, end-of-line reductions, second-hand and the like.

A typical 'save versus splurge' resolution might sound like this: 'I will indulge in these Louis Ghost Chairs' – $530 each from Kartell (spacefurniture.com.au) – 'but save by going with a mid-priced dining table, glassware or paint.' On that note, Taubmans (taubmans.com.au) are doing unbelievably good colours. Their Blackcurrant and Night Shade are great matches for the wall in this room – you could try one as a feature wall.

Once you've assessed the elements that will make or break the room, broker a deal with yourself: 'I'll skimp on the bedside tables so I can really go for it on the curtains.' There's no standard recipe for a room's success – it simply takes time, no matter what your budget.

And there are no rules, or even guidelines, for mixing. It's an intuitive process and the results are completely subjective. Most things are better when paired unexpectedly. How else do you explain why a Chinese cabinet can look so right in a 1950s setting? Or why a group of porcelain birdies bought for small change at a flea market achieves near-stunning status when put on an investment-priced side table?

Here are some great starting pieces for mixing it up:

- Kartell Bookworm from Top 3 by Design (top3design.com.au).
- Edit booklamp from Edit (edit-group.com.au).
- Syntes Skiss glass bowls from Ikea (ikea.com.au).
- Assorted chairs from Armchair (thearmchair.com.au).
- Pearl, a solid-timber ten-seater dining table from Zuster (zuster.com.au).
- Bongo stools, available in beautiful, solid colours from Korban/Flaubert (korbanflaubert.com.au), perfect for extra seating and bolts of colour at either end of the table.

Going Scandi

Every house I visited on a recent trip to Scandinavia was contained, neat, effortless and pure, but there was still enough room for individual style to come through. Scandinavians consider design to be a vital part of life and are well aware of its advantages. It was almost unnerving how beautiful everything (and everybody!) seemed to be.

Looking to Scandinavia for design cues is a sensible direction for Australian decorators to take. We share gorgeous light and a general love of the great outdoors. Their real nous comes into play, though, in the area of small spaces, something about which we have a lot to learn. They're simply magicians in the proficient use of space – how else do you explain the flat, pre-packed genius of Ikea? The region also lays claim to the world's biggest names in design: Karl Andersson, Piet Hein, Arne Jacobsen, Henrik Thor-Larsen, Bruno Mathsson, Eva Solo and Hans Wegner, to name just a few.

Sustainability is a major concern for Scandinavians, and they apply it not only to their general living but also their design aesthetic. They don't feel the need to fill their spaces with loads of comforting clutter, because their rooms are generally geared to appreciating the outdoors. This means that they don't change their rooms or furniture all the time like we do. Pieces are bought (and built) for lifetimes, not quick fixes.

A Scandi homeowner will more often than not arrange their chairs to face the windows and, despite their winters, have very little in the way of curtains. Their homes are always heated and they like to witness the weather in all its glory, no matter what the season. This also lets them be the first to welcome guests and encourages at-home entertaining.

When taking your cues from the masters, consider the following:

- With larger furniture pieces (tables, chairs, sides and lounges), choose one colour and stick to it. The real beauty lies in the honesty of the materials.
- Limed, light, milk-washed or light grey floors are typical of the Scandi sensibility and work beautifully with their furniture.
- If you're working with more of an antique look, washed-out florals, stripes and soft checks can look amazing among the 'shabbier' traditional furniture.
- The colour palette for the overall furnishings works best in the softer tones: think eggshell, latte, stone, string, with hints of soft reds, pinks, greens and blues.
- Try marrying old pieces with new – aged and patina-ed pieces can look even more stunning when paired with sleeker mid-twentieth-century designs.

Shock their socks off!

One of Diana Vreeland's personal pronouncements was: 'We all need a splash of bad taste . . . No taste is what I'm against.' In a time when complete cookie-cutter looks for a room can be bought off the furniture-store floor, Ms Vreeland's sentiment could not be more modern. Doing your own bad taste rather than someone else's version of good taste is always the better option.

There are plenty of reasons why we want to live among design and decorating that is supposedly 'in good taste'. Many homeowners justify their rather sedate choices by saying that they're 'best for resale' or 'what the market wants'. Others are just too scared to try anything outside the square. The most interesting thing about working in interiors is that you realise how completely subjective is good taste. One person's lack of taste is another person's masterpiece.

'Shocking' is a style I love to try at any given opportunity. It's the territory where conformity is a crime and the only faux pas is dressing down your space. Usually reserved for hip hoteliers, events designers and mad art collectors who live in premium apartment buildings, shocking can also work well in our day-to-day rooms, adding incredible impact, just like the foyer of a fabulous hotel. Best of all, it requires nothing much more than a badge of bravery. A touch of shock can help an otherwise uninteresting room take flight, or take an already character-filled room to another level. And here's a tip: shocking rooms are usually based on triadic contrasts – such as three colours from the colour wheel that are equidistant from each another.

Shocking can also be the result of a major art purchase; while it goes against the basics of room-planning, I do believe it's worthwhile only starting to decorate a room once you've chosen and fallen in love with the artwork for it. It will act as the room's major focal point, from which you'll easily be able to conceive all the room's other elements. Some people have already finished the room and are just waiting to find the suitable painting for above the lounge or mantelpiece. This, however, reduces their chance of any real success in locating the 'right' piece. Starting by visiting galleries and exhibitions is much the easier way. Furniture, paint colours and decorative elements can easily be colour-matched (or mismatched) to a painting, but it's pretty tricky to work in the opposite direction.

So, in the words of Ms Vreeland, 'Never fear being vulgar, just boring.'

Avoid boring with one of these 'shockers':

- Bumblebee chair from Edit (edit-group.com au).
- Seed vase in Swirl Art from Dinosaur Designs (dinosaurdesigns.com.au).
- Licorice cup and saucer from Stoneage Ceramics (stoneageceramics.com).
- Greg Natale rug from Designer Rugs (designerrugs.com.au).
- Chester ottoman from Temperature Design (temperaturedesign.com.au).

Coastal comfort

Beach houses decorated all dark and serious just don't do it for me. I've seen some of the best properties made over in sombre and handsome tones, but to me it was like having the curtains drawn on a sunny day. Great beach houses aren't ever great because of their furniture; their ultimate success has more to do with their proximity to the water, their comfort for card games and their hammock.

The saddest thing ever is a beach house done by a decorator and rarely used by its owners. It just sits there, waiting for all the supposed fun it will have when its owners turn up. The idea of getting someone else to deal with a house that's meant be all about downtime is one reality of our time-poor society. In Australia, having a house in such a privileged location, with the sea as your immediate neighbour, is a glorious thing, especially if you're a good sharer.

If there were ever a foolproof style for decking out a house without the help of a design professional, it would be coastal. Of course this is only my opinion, but some of the best beach houses I've been lucky enough to see with my own eyes – such as Donna Karan's Hamptons home complete with yoga room or Ken Done's breathtakingly simple waterside studio – have some common threads:

- Non-serious curtains – Although it seems silly, a swanky window treatment never feels right in a coastal home. Ever. It's like turning up to a garden wedding in a tuxedo.
- No glass – This means for coffee tables, dining tables or major lighting fixtures. The only glass should be the beautiful windows framing the views. Stick with wood, woven materials and fabric; a medley of all three would be the dreamy decor trinity. Imagine a Mark Tuckey birch-base refectory dining table (marktuckey.com.au), Linus woven chairs from Ikea (ikea.com.au) – at $70 each get half a dozen, and a Laura Ashley – yes, Laura Ashley! – Richmond 2.5 seater sofa (lauraashley.com). Get me there.
- Right white – Paint the walls in a soft white rather than a stark, blue-based white. Too white turns a once sunny space into a clinical, hospital-like box. Try Flannel Flower from Taubmans (taubmans.com.au) – it's beach-perfect.
- Furniture position – No matter how weird it might look, always place the furniture to take advantage of the view or best vantage point. I shot a beach house once where all the designer furniture was turned in, facing a wall to create a conversation pit! I was close to tears.

Get uppity with uptown glamour

Uppity (or, to use the real US term, uptown glamour) is a timeless, almost foolproof decor strategy for the right room. Very different from being up-itself or trophy-house, uppity is smart, slick and schmick. It's the little black dress of the decor world and enables you to add as you wish once the established elements are set up.

Most successful uppity schemes are based on a monochromatic palette, but I've witnessed some sterling examples in rich browns and creams rather than black and white. (You just need a sense of drama in the colours for maximum effect.) Uptown glamour is particularly suited to terrace houses, where it can deal with multiple fireplaces in the front two conjoined rooms, or to gracious older style apartments. The style risks looking very sad and deliberate when pushed onto a modern apartment – unless done with extreme precision and professional help.

Digest these Nine Rules for Uppity that I have gleaned from friends with high ceilings:

1. Concentrate all your decorative effort into the smaller elements (teeny objects, display elements, glassware) and the larger ones (cabinetry, feature chairs, lighting). The middle elements can be slightly forgiven and forgotten.
2. Try to be as sympathetic as possible to the period of the building.
3. Be aware of what's up to scratch for putting on display and what's better kept behind those beautiful customised doors.
4. Try extra hard with your artwork selection. Go for harmony or impact. Artworks can make or break this scheme, as they're usually the only element with movement, texture, colour and mood.
5. Be prepared to spend all your leftover money on beautiful books. And I *mean* beautiful. Pacify yourself with Amazon. (It's somehow less scary spending thousands of dollars on books online. It also means that the heavy load is left to the delivery man and you can tell fibs about what's actually in the boxes when they come.)
6. Personalise it. Cookie-cutting copycats can go to town with uppity, but your own personal stamp and touches will push it beyond the ordinary.
7. Invest in one feature piece, such as a chair – not a pair if you can help it, but a single chair. Uptown can look very matchy-matchy and symmetrical, so one sole piece can throw this off and give the room the necessary twist.
8. This is no place for store-bought shelving: splurging on custom-built cabinetry is a given, and the shelving must be flush with the internal architecture.
9. A room like this that goes unused is very sad. Don't leave it for special occasions – relish it often, preferably daily, just as a real uptowner would.

Postmodern psychedelic

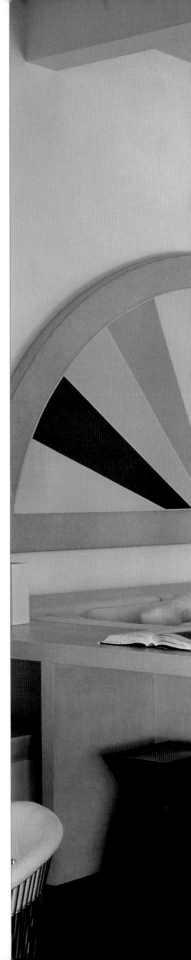

Homes that sport the postmodern style seem to say, 'Look at me, I know what I want.' The movement was built on the premise of decoration for decoration's sake, so they also seem to scream, 'I'm fun. Super fun!' They're the type of house that stays firm in their approach and they offer a confident backdrop for those who live within them.

How do you achieve this fun style yourself? The 1950s and 1960s were a time of deliberate decoration, so it's smart, savvy even, to pick up your decorative cues from them – they allow a foolproof scheme that plays dangerously within the primary colours. This is an approach with which it seems impossible to go overboard. It just seems to take more, more, more – bigger artwork, bolder statements, brighter colours, larger scale. This is a good thing, because when you're starting out, a little can really stretch a long, long way.

My favourite dealers dedicate themselves to a specific period or substyle, playing matchmaker between a piece of furniture and a client. Here is some of their advice:

- Stay true – This look relies on authenticity, which gives the room a life force all of its own. And eBay is not a sound source when it comes to securing the real deal. A copy is always a copy. When it comes to design, much of the piece's intended poetry can be lost in a watered-down faux.
- Be wise on price – Don't take a store-holder's word for it. Use your nous to find out about the maker and the piece so that you can assess its value accurately. Information is power, and a little bit of research will help you understand the price tolerance levels for originals, reissues and reproductions.
- Mind your restoration fees – If you're paying a high price, ask who restored the piece, then talk to them until you're sure you're paying for a quality restoration. Factor in a realistic restoration fee on unrestored pieces – it could be costly.
- Try full integration – Don't confine the look to one room; it works beautifully when pieces are littered throughout the home. Don't get overly hung up on 'matching' the style or materials of the pieces within your interiors.
- Make unfashionable investments – Don't buy an item simply because it's fashionable. Look out for great Australian design, quality and craftsmanship from the 1950s and 1960s.
- Consider your own comfort – If you're buying for enjoyment, not just collecting's sake, select materials that will age well, such as velvet, leather and timber.
- Watch your whites – A cool blue-based paint over a warm-based white will offset all those primary colours in a scheme like the one pictured here.

The bachelorette pad

Living as a bachelorette is something only a small handful of us will ever get to experience. The lucky members of this group live by themselves (out of choice, not situation) and are a small but smug minority. Whoever said that sharing your best things with others, compromising on just about everything, making decorative sacrifices and living under one roof was the ideal? Imagine living like a little piglet among your own things, marking out your own space and never having to ask the decorative opinion of others.

Here are some points to consider if you ever find yourself taking up residence in a bachelorette pad:

- It's the ultimate love letter to yourself, so if you love white, it must all be *blanc, blanc, blanc*, right down to the floorboards.
- These places are typically high on style, smallish on space, so go all out and wire the entire pad up with a top-of-the-line speaker system. Play it loud – people are less likely to complain when they know there's only one of you.
- No self-respecting bachelorette pad would have its television in the bedroom; this is a vulgarity reserved for married couples.
- Have as many fragrant candles as the windowsills, benchtops and bedside tables can take. I'd have about a thousand Queen B beeswax candles (queenb.com. au) illuminating every room and a dozen Diptyque Mexican Orange Blossoms (remogeneralstore.com) in the bathroom – just because I could.
- It must be extremely well insulated *and* incredibly well ventilated. Know your own body temperature and accommodate its every heating and cooling whim.
- It's mandatory to have a king-sized bed.
- Resist the urge to purchase a laundry basket. Why would you when you can just throw it straight into the machine?
- Never have just one bedside table. Fill the other one with back-up mineral water, macaroons or chick lit if you like. And dress it as nicely as you do your bedside table number one.
- Don't be a stickler for rules. If you want to recline on a series of floor cushions, so be it. If others have standard pendants, why not have a six-feet-tall shell chandelier drop?
- Personal space is the ultimate in luxury, so even if you're a hoarder, retain a little void where the eye can rest.

Bachelorettes take note: recycle like a zealot and work super hard to reduce your carbon footprint. Not only will it make you feel like a powerful single unit of change, but it will also atone for the drain on resources that living alone entails.

The movie as inspiration

I watch every movie with a great house in it a minimum of twice: once as a normal person would and then round two with the sound muted. I can then sit, fast-forward and freeze-frame it on any dreamy room set. People gush over Stokesay Court, the Jacobean-revival beauty in *Atonement*. The more universal winner, though, is Diane Keaton's living room in *Something's Gotta Give*, with its over-plumped lounges and perfect piping.

What I love about fabulous movie decors is that they're pure evidence a style works:

- *The Royal Tenenbaums* – See zebra wallpaper, fabulous family portraiture up stairways and dinky bunk beds – almost all in the one scene.
- *Amélie* – Audrey Tatou's bedroom walls seem to be one part cherry, two parts pomegranate. The best match I've found (and, trust me, I've looked high and low) is Earthen Red 107/25, hand mixed by Bauwerk (bauwerk.com.au).
- *Charade* – Audrey Hepburn's wardrobes alone make this glamorous whodunit worth watching. Seriously impressive joinery. Show your cabinetmaker now!
- *Pillow Talk* – Doris Day's apartment looks like it's given many a modern-day American decorator ideas on how to play dress-ups for bachelorettes. See Kelly Wearstler's Groundworks fabrics on kwid.com and leejofa.com (but order through mokum.com.au) for similar styles to those seen in the film.
- *A New Leaf* – Walter Matthau's apartment is a love letter to modern design. See livingedge.com.au and spenceandlyda.com.au for all things Eames.
- *The Squid and The Whale* – Laura Linney's humble brownstone is the polar opposite. See douguponbourke.com.au for soft rustic industrial.
- *Cleo from 5 to 7* – It's the display of objects in this decoratively stark 1962 French film that makes the room so perfectly intricate beneath its banal surface. Visit haveyoumetmissjones.com.au for lovely slip-cast ceramic objects.
- *Sea Biscuit* – There's a great library here. Speak to Amos Groth from Groth & Sons (02 9907 1256) for your own replicas.
- *The Hours* – Re-create Meryl Streep's understated, flower-filled apartment by visiting cavitco.com.au for the McGuire Furniture collection.
- *All That Jazz* – If you're a warehouse-perver, then, like me, you'll love Roy Scheider's place for its lived-in modernity.
- *An American in Paris* – For the ultimate space-saving apartment, you can't go past Gene Kelly's ingenious one-room in this classic. Check out smallspacestyle. blogspot.com for more space-cheating ideas.

Bespeak bespoke and share nicely

It's way too easy to write off the bespoke (read custom-made) category as a speed-dial service only for the infinitely wealthy. Bespoke is not reserved for this demographic, although it definitely keeps it afloat – it's the territory of *anyone* who wants things that aren't the same as everyone else's. Why pay good money for a duplicate that doesn't quite work for you when you can commission your own to suit your needs perfectly without compromise?

The beautiful world of bespoke is for those who need a special size, shape, colour or style – the intricacies of today's decorative appetites can't be satisfied simply from a one-size-fits-all approach. Some have entire decors custom made, while others fill theirs out with a little off the rack and a little made to order. There are bespoke options everywhere and, just like authentic organics, all you need to do is find them.

When it comes to commissioning anything, it pays to be incredibly detailed in your request – there's nothing worse than your vision being under-realised. References will help, so cut out pictures of things you like or photocopy to your heart's content. Most specialists in the bespoke trade will offer testimonials and, if you feel so inclined, you can follow these up. Word of mouth is how bespoke survives, so it's best to keep it alive by sharing.

Shamefully, *I* used to be one of those people who had a public Rolodex and a private one. The public one was bursting with the business cards of all sorts of specialists, from house-washers (pressurecleaning.com.au) to bentwood re-caners (marlboroughantiques.com.au), leather handle-makers (Perkal Brothers, phone 02 9331 3692) and everything in between. I would, in an act of great 'generosity', offer these numbers to anyone with a decor-related request. The cards of the über-tradespeople were stashed, however, in a second secret-squirrel Rolodex, just for greedy piglet me. (This was when I was in my flicking stage – buying houses, loving them to decorative death, then flicking them on.) One day I called on Gideon, the über-painter (he had an incredible way with whites and could tell White Watsonia from Chalk USA at ten paces). Mobile dead. Tried in vain. I had kept him all to myself, but my love, and that of a small group of other secretive types, couldn't keep him afloat and he fell back into his first trade, car mechanics. Shame. My bad.

So I had no choice but to merge the contents of Rolodex 1 and 2 and learn how to share properly. The deal is to offer graciously anyone and everyone who does a good job, supersedes your expectations or brief or is just plain impressive. We must especially tell everyone we know if they're exceptional and have gone out on a limb to specialise in one particular area. There are lots of jacks-of-all-trades, but not many true masters of one. Decorative sharing is the best karma of all. What goes around very often comes around.

Finding a life less ordinary

Setting aside budgetary or time constraints, a few things need to be aligned in order to create truly extraordinary rooms – ideas. Lots of people have a shoebox or clippings folder full of references, tear sheets and ever-hopeful ideas for their dream space. I'm so completely psyched by the contents of my own clippings folder that I don't even have to open it any more to get my heart racing – a look in its direction is enough.

But the most effective way to conjure inspiration or plump up your clippings folder is to skip online. (This will also keep your mags intact and shelf-worthy.) As the glossies scamper to compete with the breadth and scope of images that websites can deliver less judiciously and free of charge, more and more sites are born, just adding to the impressive number of idea-generating blogs. What I love about them is the way they can be problem- and/or room-specific (itsknotwoodblogspot.com, for example, is for anyone whose thing is faux wood).

Here are my favourite blog sites – these guys are lively, diligent and ready to share:

- apartmenttherapy.com – Enjoy entire house tours embarrassment-free – alert all the housey nosey parkers you know.
- booksathome.blogspot.com – If you're a book-lover, consider this your porn.
- habituallychic.blogspot.com – These people understand that their job is to match beautiful imagery with concise on-trend musings.
- mocoloco.com – Modernist houses, products and ideas under the stealth editing of Harry Wakefield.
- desiretoinspire.blogspot.com – An Australian (Jo) and a Canadian (Kim) take it in turns here to blog on houses.
- designspongeonline.com – Star blogger Grace Bonney offers insightful podcasts with a medley of under-the-radar and well-known interior and design talents.
- stylesavestheworld.blogspot.com – 'Be glam. Live green' is their tag, so expect eco-related ideas, sans the smugness.
- remodelista.com – Trust the no-nonsense discerning duo of Julie Carlson and Francesca Connolly to uncover the best fittings, tapware, styling tips, paint combinations and merchandise.
- decorno.blogspot.com – Blogger Elaine Miller has a take-no-prisoners style, with post titles like 'Does this chandelier make me look fat?'.
- thehousethata-mbuilt.blogspot.com – Reading this blogger's diary of renovation muck-ups has a thank-God-it's-not-me, calming effect!

Blogging is all about sharing, so if there are any blogs that you love, please send them to me: megan@meganmorton.com.

Go modern with retro

Some people are addicted to a certain era, and while it's admirable in its way, there's always something a little sad about it. Maybe it was the best time of their life, but let's be reasonable. My best time by far was when I was tall, skinny as a banister with peroxide hair and nineteen, but do you see me prancing around in a Molly dress and jelly shoes?

Mixing and referencing eras is all about perspective, and retro gives a nod to the past but has a hand in the future. We love its reliable colour palettes and familiar lines, its no-nonsense functionality and its generous and forgiving curves, its handsome wood grains, polished textures and neat-as-a-pin proportions. It makes modern pieces look better and, when paired with pieces of its own ilk, can make a room feel like an old friend.

Our appetite for retro-inspired pieces seems insatiable and I think a lot of it has to do with the sweet innocence this period represents. It was decorative for decoration's sake, and a time of real pride in all matters of the home.

Retro pieces are best when incorporated within a broader scheme. While I love the form of the seating options of the period, I find their comfort levels not up to scratch with today's standards, so I love using retro chairs as hero or feature chairs rather than relying on a whole suite for seating. I've found fabulous one-offs at angelucci.net.au.

The best way to create retro is with wall decorations, lighting and objects, mixing them with modern-day repros of lounges and dining chairs. Genuine retro dining tables, especially those with additional leaves, are space-savingly fabulous and relatively cheap (see classicaldanishfurniture.com or danishvintagemodern.com.au). I've seen a lot of retro pieces bastardised by inappropriate upholstery fabrics. By all means re-cover it, but use a modern-day fabric in a colour suitable to the era (try kvadratmaharam.com).

Here are a few basics rules you should bear in mind with retro:

- Multiples – At the time, people only ever used multiples of small accessories. And even then they wouldn't have been same-same but similar.
- Proportions – High ceilings were not common in new 1950s housing; a twisting bulbous retro light works beautifully in a high-ceilinged room from an earlier era.
- Colour – Yellow. It acts as a full stop and complements the earthy wooden tones. Sparingly used, yellow and teal blue add authenticity and a dash of pop.
- Flooring – The 1950s to 1970s were a time of debauched lifestyles, so retro rugs are not really worth preserving for reasons of hygiene alone (unless they're the almost museum-piece ones from 506070.com.au)! Pair your mid-century sofa with a new pile rug and voilà – you're ever so modern.

Should you buy the fake or the real deal? Buying a replica of something is a little bit like singing your favourite song at karaoke. The song runs at about eleven per cent likeness, and it's hard even to sound your usual best. European copyright laws are stringent against anyone caught selling a reproduction, but in Australia we love all the cheap things we can get from China and offer designers no such protection. You get what you pay for, but sometimes not even. The problem, too, is that the asking price of the copies is usually not eleven per cent of the original price tag anyway; they're greedily more like fifty per cent! Before you buy, just consider singing 'Islands in the Stream' on a karaoke mike. I've tried as both Dolly and Kenny and it's really hard – that majority percentage really does matter!

Relax, it's casual

Many people assume that casual means low end, but let me tell you, there's nothing low rent about casual. When done well, it's ridiculously comfortable, effortlessly stylish and works incredibly well with the Australian way of life. There are many international designers who hang their hat on casual. Take India Hicks, for instance – it's not just her home style, casual is her way of life. Locally, the epitome of casual chic is the incredibly beautiful, handcrafted aesthetic that Lee Mathews brings to fashion and a small range of homewares.

I've noticed that the best casual rooms don't follow any particular recipe – it comes down to the room's pared-back formation. Interested in attempting your own version? Well, the good news is that casual rooms usually only have casual owners – anyone too wound up won't appreciate this style's honest nature. The best way to start is to include only furniture that the room needs – overstuffing the space with unnecessary elements takes away from the whole intention of casual. Whether it's a bedroom, kitchen or living room, stick to the bare necessities. When it comes to the lounge itself, even a stitched-up one can be taken down a notch or two if it's draped in a throw or piled up with cushions that have tassels, threads or texture.

Maintain the integrity of casual by opting for open shelving with simple lines rather than intricate and complex storage units. Staying committed to one colour palette will also help. Contrary to popular belief, a casual room can do just as well in darks as it can in whites; dark wood and darker stained floors can really work when it comes to casually dressing down.

I find that, while this look can tolerate cheaper chain-store items, it does better when the room's decorative elements come from pieces of noticeably good quality. The more pared-down you go, the better each element probably needs to be. (This is why it's so much easier to dress a cluttered space within a tight budget, because with everything packed in your eyes tend to notice only the room as a whole, rather than each individual el-cheapo item.)

Bear in mind, though, that not everyone can do casual. It doesn't sit too well with overwhelming amounts of technology, built-in cabinetry or imposing artworks. It's main goals are to comfort and cocoon you, which might go a long way to explaining the perennial affection in which we hold hideaway holiday shacks that look like laid-back beach houses – the sort of place whose humble offerings would have luxury hotel managers shaking their five-star heads in wonder. The best thing about casual rooms is that they know all too well that it's their owners, their friends and their guests that bring in all the energy and life.

Here are three casual but chic options to try:

1. A vintage floral quilt from Empire Vintage (empirevintage.com. au).
2. Antique ceramic jugs from Butterfield Tate Gallery (hazelbutterfieldtate. com).
3. A Tripod Light from Studio Ham (studioham.com.au).
4. Rustic tinware and baskets from Perfect Pieces (perfectpieces. com.au).
5. Indoor–outdoor wicker pieces from Mandalay Designs (mandalaydesigns. com.au).

Express yourself in the bedroom

Show me the bedroom and I'll show you the person. Going from house to house, I find the best way to understand the homeowner in question is to spec their master suite first – a bedroom is like a window into the real person behind the house. Not only do you get a quick glimpse into their colour preferences and their favourite things, their true cleaning nature will also become obvious.

Letting your personality shine through is the joy of working on your bedroom, so how do you find your decorative self to begin with? Sure, you're good at your day job and know your stuff, but how can your bedroom be the authentic 'room' version of you? One really effective way to get some kind of idea is undertake the shoebox challenge.

Over a period of six months (this can be shorter, but the more time you have to dwell on it, the better), consciously fill a shoebox with the things that resonate with you – tile samples, paint chips, magazine pages, photocopies. When your box is ready, hand it over to your designer or to yourself and they or you will have a highly personal starting point for the project at hand. Some people have handed me their boxes with an egg carton in it – an egg carton in just the right shade can in fact be a beautiful reference point for interior wall colours.

Here are some things to consider when getting to know your interior self:

- When you're tearing pages out of magazines, it might not be clear to you what it is about the room that you like. Don't over-analyse it – it's usually the overall mood of the room that appeals to you.
- Collect as many paint chips as take your fancy then narrow them down to three and request sample pots so you can test them on your walls.
- Go on a rampage with your digital camera. Take shots of friends' furniture, fabrics, doorknobs and cupboard profiles that you like. Your photos will prove invaluable when trying to explain to tradespeople exactly what it is you're trying to create. Profile shots of cabinetry are extremely helpful for showing your cabinetmaker the proportions you want.
- Include items that represent the colour you're trying to achieve. Someone once gave me a photo of a beautiful vintage green car, the only match they could find for the slightly dirty green they were after. We took it to the paint shop and had it computer colour-matched. In short, nothing is too silly. Nothing.
- Try apartmenttherapy.com for some real-life examples of rooms that work.
- This is not copy-catting. The idea is to have a piece of evidence that what you were hoping for works. From there you can add your own touches and nuances.

Taking inspiration from history

My husband (chalk) is a history nut and I (cheese) am not. What I have discovered, merely through association, is that there are some satisfying lessons to be learnt by way of decoration. For instance, what were the mad Victorians thinking when they put toilets in outhouses? And how beautifully appointed was the English Georgian style? The honest proportions of the rooms, the humble decadence of the lifestyle expressed in small-scale but usually narrative artwork, and the deft hand with greys and other subdued colours are just dead impressive.

Sometimes I think I was not meant to live in this day and age. I would have preferred the house of an overindulged Elizabethan – as long as I could swap to the colour-drenched low-line appointments of the 1950s for my weekender. We're so spoilt for choice these days, with centuries of good and bad design from which to make our selection. Bringing out the best for modern living is not just a matter of choosing the right colours, it's also about taking the right eras and intermixing them confidently.

I never like to completely replicate a period in the one room (unless my client is a total history nut or a slave to one decade). Instead, my suggested ratio is about two parts period to five parts modern. I work out the proportions by concentrating on five elements: floors and rugs, lounge and furniture, window dressings, artworks and architecture.

Designers are forever drawing on the past to refresh the future, so I asked some famed design professionals what history lessons they like best:

- Melbourne interior designer Mardi Doherty (dohertylynch.com) thanks the Victorians for teaching us that a high ceiling can make a house cooler in summer. She also loves the 1950s for their appreciation and understanding of the sun's orientation, and for their coloured laminates and moulded plastics.
- Mike Dawborn, a 1950s, 1960s and 1970s specialist (506070.com.au), speaks of the new materials, such as plastic, that were put to use in these eras. He also mentions the highly sculptural shapes that the new plastics and foams afforded.
- Frank and Georgina Howell of Howell & Howell (howell-howell.com) prefer the early eighteenth century, inspired by the excavation of Pompeii. This gave us neoclassical style, which meant the return of asymmetry and straighter-than-straight lines.
- Rachel Castle, a homewares designer (castleandthings.com.au) cites Bauhaus for its gift of black, yellow, red and blue, and its discipline with structure.
- Ros Palmer, the antiques queen (rospalmerinteriors.com), admires eras that ooze romance: 'I like to design rooms with a heart beat and that always lean on historic precedent.'

Want to press pause to see some historical rooms? Check out these films:

- *Dangerous Liaisons* – A perfect house inhabited by oversexed, spoilt-brat aristocrats. Get inspired for a decadent dinner party.
- *Quo Vadis* – See Rome and its homes as well as a young Peter Ustinov.
- *Miss Pettigrew Lives for a Day* – Enjoy decadent penthouse living, a great vestibule filled with wall sconces and some fab bed heads in this love letter to the 1930s.
- *Elizabeth* – Cate Blanchett was really meant to have lived in the sixteenth century. Lay it on, Lizzie.
- *Little Miss Sunshine* – A great ad for panelled wood and pot plants. Okay, it's not decorative at all, but it's too funny not to include.
- *Marie Antoinette* – Has there ever been a better dressed or panelled boudoir? I think not. Thank you, Sophia C., for concentrating as hard on the chateau dressings as the clothing.

Overindulge – go on!

Going over the top is what some interior designers do best. They do it because their colour-loving client gives them complete carte blanche and wants to be taken somewhere they aren't capable of going themselves. In my opinion, the world already has enough safe and boring houses that are the epitome of good taste. Let's welcome in overindulgence.

Much like the spoilt only child, the overindulged room gets whatever it calls for. And in the spirit of dutiful decorating, this can be anything from Murano glass chandeliers to imported yellow velvet. The key to overindulging a room is special, one-off pieces – and, basically, there's a world shortage of these.

Here's a list of specialty stores committed to unearthing the most flamboyant and fabulous items (keep it close – a dining-room makeover might be nearer than you think, and it takes only one piece to get the ball rolling):

- Mondo Trasho – Never, I repeat, never say you'll think about it and come back later if you find something here you like. Trust me, it won't be there the next day. 387 Johnston Street, Abbotsford Vic. 3067, (03) 9486 9595 (mondotrasho.com.au).
- Parterre Garden – You'll find chandeliers here that really are from French ballrooms. Even the dust here is authentic. 33 Ocean Street, Woollahra NSW 2025, (02) 9363 5874 (parterre.com.au).
- Laura Kincade – She does great rococo bed heads and four-poster canopy beds. 80 O'Riordan Street, Alexandria NSW 2015, (02) 9667 4415 (laurakincade.com).
- The Bitch is Back – These are pieces with big personalities and rightly so – most of them are design blue bloods. 100A Barkly Street, St Kilda Vic. 3182, (03) 9534 8025 (thebitchisback.com.au).
- Becker Minty – Their boxy velvet single chair, ridiculously luxurious possum rugs, deer heads and mounted butterflies are spot on – the epitome of indulgence. 81 Macleay Street (enter Manning Street), Potts Point NSW 2011, (02) 8356 9999 (beckerminty.com).
- Chuck & Bob – Everything here looks like it needs a super-large room. 2–14 Amelia Street, Waterloo NSW 2017, (02) 9699 2117.
- Edit – Here you'll find lights that look like they have ball gowns on, chairs that look like people, and objects that are never what they seem. 146 Foveaux Street, Surry Hills NSW 2010, (02) 9358 5806 (edit-group.com.au).

Here are some great sites for online overindulgence:

- 1stdibs.com – You can't go past the eye-goggling buys available here. It makes eBay look like a bad suburban garage sale.
- jfchen.com – Another dealer trading in ridiculously decadent feature pieces. Spend up big!
- hermes.com – The ultimate online service from the world's most luxurious house. Although heavy in fashion accessories, the site also trades in porcelain cups and saucers, trays and other indulgences. Small things (when they come in an orange box) can make big gestures.

Contemplating wabi-sabi

The perfect plastic world we live in leaves us all in the sweetest position to appreciate wabi-sabi, a decorative philosophy based on small pleasures rather than showy gains, one that honours the handcrafted and all its imperfections. This Japanese aesthetic, based on the acceptance of impermanence, gently celebrates the austere, the imperfect and the modest.

The poet Matsuo Bashō is credited with combining the words *wabi* ('lonely') and *sabi* ('rust') to explain 'the taste for the simple and the quiet'. The true gift of wabi-sabi is its appreciation of reduction, and of the dignity and honesty of a space and its contents.

Wabi-sabi is never messy – cleanliness implies respect. Worn things take on a magic only in a setting where it's clear they cannot harbour dirt or grime! The reason they've survived to bear the marks of time is that they've been so well cared for through the years.

Doling out tips for wabi-sabi is like trying to teach universal peace, but it's an intrinsically easy concept to grasp. It comes from a resistance to decoration and attention to the simple elements that make up a room, including the voids between them. It's a beautiful thing to be aware of, especially in lean times. Try taking a close look at the form, material and design of single pieces, rather than the effect the pieces have collectively.

These products, deliberately or by accident, are all informed by the theory of wabi-sabi:

- Touch Me bed linen – Crumply linen from Ivano Redaelli that refuses even to have any closures at the bottom of the doona cover. Try the tea-stained number 12 (no names, just numbers). Prices from $380 (for a pair of pillowcases) and $1362 (for a doona cover) at Hub Furniture, (03) 9652 1222 (hubfurniture.com.au).
- Wooden Stools by Jo Wilson – These smoothed wooden toadstools are ideal for bedsides, spare seating and coffee tables. Prices from $590 to $690 at Planet Furniture, (02) 9211 5959 (planetfurniture.com.au).
- Dint vases by Deb Jones – The subtle, nipped-in dimpling of these one-offs makes them a gentle way to show off the simplest flowers. Prices from $530 at Planet Furniture, (02) 9211 5959 (www.planetfurniture.com.au).
- Slab End dining table and bench seat – Former wharf timber planks are finished with rusted-steel detail; leave them outside to weather for ever and ever. Get them at Mark Tuckey, (03) 9419 3418 (marktuckey.com.au).
- Porcelain mug by Sandy Lockwood – Sandy partners earthy stoneware with salt-glazed porcelain for that elusive truthfulness. Her attempts to express the transience of life and the delicacies of nature are the essence of wabi-sabi. You'll find them at All Hand Made Gallery, (02) 9386 4099 (allhandmadegallery.com).

Creating drama in black and white

Is there any other colour combination that can be positively hypnotic in one room and then all suave and sophisticated in another? Black and white is the Clydesdale of the colour wheel, one of the hardest working colour combinations in existence. It just gives so much back. Not just for solo performances, black and white also seems to have super powers when combined with any other colour. Challenge it. It's hard to find a colour that doesn't work with it.

Black is as complex as white. Van Gogh claimed to have identified twenty-seven shades of black in the paintings of Franz Hals. In fact, the monochromatic palette of many of the Dutch masters can be so inspirational – lace collars over black velvets, black-and-white checked floors. All my favourite designers and decorators, both past (Billy Baldwin, David Hicks) and present (Kelly Wearstler, Ian Halliday), employ the graphic capabilities of black and white to underpin most of their schemes. Wearstler says, 'Black-and-white lines have graphic power on their own, but reworked as a hound's-tooth-plaid pillow, a geometric band on a curtain or a zebra-skin rug, those same lines feel sophisticated and smart.'

Now that's a great idea! If the complete wall-to-floor coverage of black and white scares you, try it in smaller, punctuating doses, such as a floor covering, window treatment or bed dressing. And if they still seem far too bold, attempt even smaller portions – on a table top or a mantelpiece.

Black and white might feel like a brave choice, but in fact it's perfect for decorative virgins, the lazy or scaredy cats. Once you put the basic black-and-white components in place, there's not much left to do – they'll do all the work for you. If you want to play within the boundaries of black and white, mix your greys with highlights of shimmer and shine. In small doses, silver, titanium, stainless steel and chrome are all perfect for softening as well as playing up to the sexiness of black and white. They're the sure-fire way to modernise this design classic.

Consider these points when choosing black-and-white colour combos:

- Mid-brown won't work with black and white – it comes over all Old Aunty. Dark brown wood is the only exception here.
- Black and white against red is modernity personified.
- Orange adds a surprising retro turn.
- Purple provides pure decadence.
- Beige is so quietly elegant.
- Green adds an injection of freshness.
- Grey, as seen here, is devastatingly handsome.

attention to detail

Wood works

In a world where it's usual for people to pay double digits for tea towels, wood proves itself over and over again as a smart choice. In this white-box world of ours, it's common to encounter resistance to the natural charms of wood. But let's do a U-turn and reconsider wood's incredible beauty – just think how its natural tones can enhance the atmosphere of an otherwise ho-hum room.

Although wood is a reliable material that decorators have put to work for centuries, most modern homes have cleared out the wood to make way for contemporary white replacements. Why? Well, wood can be difficult to deal with – variations in tone and conflicting textures can make it tricksy. Let's face it, with all those different hues and grains, it's a bit like attempting to decorate a room in seventeen different shades of yellow. Not an easy feat!

Unless you have panache for French oak or an inheritance's worth of rosewood, it's advisable to use only small injections of wood for maximum appeal. Applying it in smaller doses is a time-tested strategy that can deliver great results. You know that feeling when you walk into a room and you can't quite work out what it is about it that makes it so lovely? A closer inspection of the elements will more than likely reveal the warmth of wood. A time-worn dining table can bring the most over-designed, elite dining chairs down a peg, while a wooden side table can add that missing element of charm to any room. Watch the magic happen when a wooden chair joins a room. Voilà – instant honesty and warmth.

When it comes to placing wood, you'll notice that it has a natural attraction to most other natural elements. Bamboo, stone, woven fibres, rope detailing, water hyacinth and shells all seem to work brilliantly in its company. These natural pieces appear to have the same effect as a little dash of red in a room – stunning. And then there's the general recycling process that choosing to live with wooden furniture entails.

Found something woody but unsure what sort it is? Want to know what wood is what? Contact Jugo Ilic at knowyourwood@bigpond.com. He's smart and has superior knowledge when it comes to wood. Failing that, *Wood: Identification & Use* by Terry Porter is great reference for DIY identification.

Hanging with the French

Sport and politics aside, the French really know how to do things well. Take, for example, their supremacy when it comes to the decorative world. Not a season goes by without a French influence somewhere. Style seems to be part of their birthright and, as a nation, they're responsible for the best homeware trends. Not only that, but they consider all *objets trouvés* to be important, they tend not to get fat while baking brioche effortlessly and their language is musical. The French expression for window-shopping is *lècher les vitrines*. It might not be the most beautiful of phrases, but its literal translation is to 'to lick the windows' and, let's face it, shopping in Paris is positively drool-worthy.

Two other divine little inventions we have to thank the French for are the art of display and the knack of knick-knacking. We all know that their artists are masters of large-scale works of major importance, but at the other end of the scale the French have also perfected the art of placing smaller pieces on a wall. Known as the 'French hang', it basically consists of putting diminutive works in mixed media together on the one wall. Widely used today in hotels and chic houses, its origins lie in Parisian cafes. Legend has it that struggling artists of the likes of Matisse and Renoir used to paint or sketch small works and give them to the cafe proprietors in return for F & B. It proved to be a win-win. Artists were nourished and the cafe walls were full of small canvases that made for an energetic and interesting mix.

Tim Olsen recommends the French hang as a great way to enter the art market, investing in several smaller pieces rather than larger ones. Decorator Tina de Salis says it's the perfect way to unify a large space by adding smaller components. What everyone agrees on is how the French hang can work to hold together so many styles, genres and artists. Some people prefer to keep a general theme running through the single elements – such as a similar colour or subject matter – but in the best ones I've seen, caution has been thrown to the wind and the wall acts as a rarefied pin board. The French hang pictured here is a great example of anything goes. Graphically interesting images with a monochromatic theme are expertly framed on a green background. Clever.

The best thing about the French hang is the way it can accommodate your three-year-old's finger painting as well as your Whiteley etching – the wall acts as one big equaliser. Sometimes having all the same frames helps give the collection some consistency, but otherwise it's your chance to have your own little mini gallery. Try it in a room that needs personalising. And if you stick to smaller works, you'll have no trouble moving them around. Another win-win!

The best place to see the French hang in a modern setting is Kate Spade's Soho Store (454 Broome Street, New York, NY 10013). Here you'll find a collection of wonderful prints, framed book covers, paintings and drawings that would look equally good in your own large room. It hits the spot and shows exactly how it's done.

WEST NO 2 BOX

AND BURWOOD DEPOT
AND CUMBERLAND HIGH SCHOOL
AND DRUMMOYNE AV
AND LEICHHARDT DEPOT
AND RYDE DEPOT
RACECOURSE
SCHOOL
SHOWGROUND
SPECIAL
ENTWORTH PARK
SHFIELD
T AND SPORTS GROUNDS
XPRESS
ROLD PARK
USTRIAL
CHARTER
OU ENTER
-FIVEDOCK
CANTERBURY

legends

Miller   MARTIN HARRISON

ULTIMATE STYLE

SHOTS OF STYLE

THE PRIVATE WORLD OF THE DUKE AND DUCHESS OF WINDSOR

THE MAGIC

THE NECKLACE

ANNIE LEIBOVITZ WOMEN SUSAN SONTAG

Wallpaper redux

Florence Broadhurst, were she still alive today, should be awarded an Order of Australia. Yes, Ms B. was in fact a true-blue Australian, despite the fact that most Australians – due to her ahead-of-her-timeness – thought she was some highly talented, still-living European textile designer when her designs creations were first re-released by Signature Prints (signatureprints. com.au) six years ago.

If you look closely, of course, there's not a waratah or bottlebrush in sight in her wallpaper designs. Instead she offered seductive swirls, rushes of stallions, ribbons of gold and motifs that still have as transcendental an effect as they did back in 1969. Some people are so taken with her work that they camouflage entire rooms by applying the one print in both wallpaper and fabric. Others use small but deliberate placements simply to pep up a room, or larger splashes to create a talking point.

Feted around the world, she can be credited with the resurgence of wallpaper; the only shame is that she's not here to witness the divine fruits of her labours. She sexied up wallpaper's image, which then led to established European houses re-releasing traditional designs – to the applause of the modern decorator. The best thing, though, about the rise and rise of wallpaper is the way it's now viewed as an alternative to a painted wall in all rooms of the house, no longer stuck in the main living room and on show to all. I think one of the best ways to put the decorative charms of wallpaper to use is in the smaller rooms or secret-squirrel locations – somewhere you'd least expect it, such as the bathroom. But don't just stop there: think of children's rooms – Anna French's Cloud paper is exceptionally dreamy for nurseries – or libraries and studies – where Brunschwig & Fils Bibliotheque is an obvious but never boring choice.

Select small spots that could do with some spunk. One clever friend has papered just the doors of her wardrobe in her own family crest from custom-maker kgdesigns.com.au – with spectacular success. The clever wife of another friend has papered one wall in her kitchen with the one-day-to-a-page leaves from a Chinese calendar. I love the idea of running a roll of Taylor and Wood's Frames, available at Chee Soon & Fitzgerald (you can draw, doodle and defame within these frames once the paper is hung) to the back of a door. (Check Frames out at grahambrown.com.)

Next time you're overhauling, don't overlook wallpaper's charms and don't be put off the two-part wallpaper-application process. I find that hanging it can be quietly satisfying, but don't even get me started on what the removal process is like. A word of warning: if you own a house that was built in 1959ish, the stripping is one job to delegate. They were really into it back then, and I can safely bet you it will be at least three layers thick!

For a Chinese calendar like the one pictured here, try Remo (remogeneralstore. com). They sell the standard colour print on white A4 sheets. I've framed the dates of my children's birthdays and made fab oversized cards from the unused dates.

Displaying your photographs

It's a personal choice whether you display the most memorable moments of your nearest and dearest on a wall. In my line of work, I'm sometimes taken aback at the level of, let's say, intimacy that people are willing to share with complete strangers and visitors through their photo arrangements.

On the whole, though, framed photographs are very beautiful things. They can define a space and give telltale signs of the occupants' loves and lives. There are ways, however, to make them even more beautiful. Let's deal with the practical side first. Assuming you've already gone to the effort of taking your favourite images to the framer (insist on UV-absorbing glass or acrylic, otherwise you can expect sun damage), and you've managed to gathered up a hammer and nail, now put everything down before you get nail happy. Replace all that with a pencil, scissors and paper. Trace the frames you wish to display on the wall and cut them out of the paper. Play with the positions of the paper copies on the wall by sticking them down with Blu-Tack, making sure you keep sufficient space between them and moving them around until you've found the ideal hanging arrangement. (Real hanging purists make actual colour photocopies of their framed works so they can consider the colours and composition as well as space.) Once you've got your ideal layout, keep the paper copies on the wall as guides until you bang that nail in, then remove them when the real frame is about to go up. I can't guarantee you un-wonky frames, but I can guarantee you perfect positions every time.

Now as far as the actual content goes, scale usually plays a big part in the success of the overall effort. Putting a small photograph in an oversized frame, for example, is a great way to draw attention to it or create a focal point. Filling a frame edge to edge and top to toe with a favourite image has the same high-impact result. Some people have great success in keeping all their frames the same and grouping together photos with matching content, such as black-and-white moments, for example, but my feeling is this approach can be just like a Vegemite sandwich – classic, reliable but a tad ho-hum. A more random, unexpected approach will give a glimpse of your personality. And this is pretty much what you get, in the end, when you frame as you go, mixing professionally framed shots with cheap tricks.

What I do detest are the latest digital photo frames that click over a range of chosen pictures all the time. Are we that tied to technology that we need it to flip the pages of our photo albums for us? Riffle through last year's top snaps and take them to your local framer pronto. And if putting your life on display for all to see is not your cup of tea, there are plenty of archive-quality storage boxes, journals and albums to maintain your privacy.

The best, most reliable arrangement I've seen is a line-up of favourite people, with all the portraits shot from the same distance. This repetitive format maintains interest and the similar focus allows each face or scene to shine. Digitally printed canvases can also be stunning – try liveprint.com.au or domayne.com.au.

The perfect display

There's a divine little book by Leonard Koren called *Arranging Things: The Rhetoric of Object Placement*, a poetic journey through one man's obsession with the positions of things. It investigates the 'coupling' of objects, and goes on to dissect superb ideas describing the magic that happens when certain things sit together on a mantelpiece or a shelf. It was recommended to me by another stylist and I've loved every single page of it – so much so that I had to buy another copy on Amazon so I could have one for good and one for page-tagging and defacing.

Sometimes the best houses in the world have the most uninspiring displays, while the simplest of homes can create complete and utter magic. There is, then, no real relationship between money and quality of display. The really impressive arrangements take shape, colour and texture as their muse. Any surface can offer a display space, from the smallest of sills to the grandest of mantels. If you're new to the displaying gig, practise all you like, but be warned, it can be a real afternoon-waster.

I practise my own often. To throw myself off, I sometimes even set myself a challenge: to incorporate that unsightly so-and-so into my display or to force that green element to work with the rest. Sad, some might say, but all too true.

Here are some simple tips to get you started, but never follow them to the letter – we all know that one person's display is another's idea of a dust trap:

- To start with, choose one thing you really adore – from a piece of art to a flower or a ceramic piece – and let it dictate the rest of your display.
- Once you're up and running, opt for a style that complements the inherent character of the space.
- If you want order and symmetry, try using two of everything, one on either side – it will work a treat.
- Use the form, shape and colour of flowers and foliage to add some interest. There's nothing more perfectly imperfect than nature.
- Consider your arrangement to be a changing tableau – nothing need be there forever and it can be added to or changed over altogether whenever you like. Such things take time and effort, but if you have enough of either, the perfect arrangement is easy to achieve and will reward you daily.

Arranging Things is by far the best book on the subject of the importance of display, but here are three more that I've enjoyed:

- Katherine Sorrell's *The Art of Display: Creating Style with Decorative Objects*, Mitchell Beazley, London, 2002.
- Stafford Cliff & Gilles de Chabaneix's *The Way We Live With the Things We Love*, Thames & Hudson, London, 2009.
- Strunk & White's *The Elements of Style*, illustrated by Maira Kalman, The Penguin Press, New York, 2005.

The magic of metallics

There are two schools of thought when it comes to putting the almost magical powers of metallics to work. One is to really floor it, take no prisoners, as here. The other is to sprinkle it sparingly – a more subtle, premium dusting. Whichever approach you decide to take, here are seven all-encompassing rules that are reliable and appropriate for both:

1. Unless you're an extremely skilled hand (I'm talking about the top one per cent of the decorating population here), resist the urge to mix your metals. This means not even the slightest crossover of silver and gold. The only exception would be the possible combination of metals with super-similar tones, such as gold with *hints* of copper, or silver with *teeny* touches of pewter.

2. Metallics have an unmatched ability to disguise or act as a band-aid to a room that might be poor in size or quality. If you go the full silver or gold floor to ceiling, the eye won't ever look up or down. It will always be entertained in the middle, where all the interesting wall treatments are.

3. Patterns tend to lead the eye around a room. A pattern within the mix (say a textured metallic wallpaper) gives the eye something to rest on and stops the scheme from feeling overly restless.

4. Silver can really work to increase the perceived size of a room. In combination with natural light, it can give marvellous results, making the room seem lighter and brighter. Gold (which works in almost the opposite way) can be perfect for adding a sense of cosiness and warmth.

5. True whites don't look their best in metallic settings, taking on a glow from the metals surrounding them and coming over slightly muddied, losing their clean, concise lines. Greys (from soft through to graphite), blacks, creams and ivories are better options.

6. The best friends of metallics in decorating circles are mirrors. Each one will basically double the effect of the metallics within the room, so use this to create high impact. Abusing it can also really work. Book-ending with mirrors (placing mirrors on either side of a section of the room) can be incredible, but just be sure you like what you see between them. Metallics might be forgiving, but mirror is a truth stick.

7. An all-metallic room will appear completely different in the morning, afternoon and evening. Do your testing at the same time you'll be using the room. Don't put up the breakfast-room paint options on a Saturday afternoon.

It's all done with mirrors

Mirrors are the key to telling decorative lies. Well, not lies as such – more like fibs. Innocent fibs. Need to make a room look bigger? Need to exude an air of sophistication? Run out of funds but need to multiply the effect of the basic elements in a room? Try mirrors.

Get inspired by mirrors by looking at their more clever commercial applications. French boutique hotels use them with great flair. Kelly Whearstler has used them with pure frivolity at The Viceroy Hotel (viceroysantamonica.com – look at the mirrored reception area in the 'Business Travel' section). And closer to home, landscape architect Annie Wilkes (parterre. com.au) uses them to multiply the symmetry of her impeccable exteriors.

Here are some tips for playing with the reflective power of the mirror for instant glamour:

- Orientation – Look very carefully at what you're reflecting and consider the reflection options from all possible hanging points in the room.
- Reflective furniture – Mirrored furniture is having its moment in the sun, but certain shapes may highlight extension cords, power points and flooring. I'd always opt for rose-stained or smoky grey tones, rather than clear mirror.
- Cleaning – Paper towel with warm water will give good results.
- Thickness – When it comes to mirrors stuck to walls, you get what you pay for. Resist the urge, though, to save some bucks, and go for a thicker, more substantial mirror. According to mostlymirrors.com.au, the minimum thickness for a wall-mounted mirror longer than half a metre should be 6 millimetres. There's an added air of class with a thicker slice anyway.
- Cost – With a less expensive mirror you can risk de-silvering in a shorter time.
- Other applications – There are lots of chandeliers and lights made out of mirror to choose from. Or Jacqueline Morony (millicent-frank.com) makes to order beautiful mirror-finished letters and shapes that are perfect on a wall.
- Covering up – Turn an imperfect wall into a feature wall by covering it entirely in mirror – you'll be surprised at its affordability and delighted with its luxe look.
- Reflection – If you've got a knockout view, don't confuse it by using multi-panelled mirror to show it off. Do it justice with a single pane.
- Instant flair – If you're trying to re-create the charm and relaxed opulence of the French or Belgian sitting room, cheat by installing a Versailles-like grid.
- Mirror and art – Placing a mirror opposite a favourite piece of artwork is effective, but be warned: it could start to feel like visual wallpaper, leaving it overexposed.

Speaking of French hotels with flair, check out the Hôtel Plaza Athénée in Paris (plaza-athenee-paris. com), the hotel used in *Sex in the City*'s 'An American Girl in Paris' episodes. They love to use mirror there, and it's generally a knockout place to stay if you're ever in town. Closer to home, have a look at the Ivy Lounge and the Den (merivale.com), where the use of etched mirror, 1950s-style, over the cabinetry is exquisite.

Flawless white floors

I can dole this information out responsibly, given I have extremely handsome dark floors (two coats of Black Japan, soaked up quickly rather than allowed to set, followed by a once-over with tung oil for a flat, matt, chalky finish) and beautiful blindingly white boards (marine-grade paint). Now, it must be said that I'd never usually subscribe to two completely different floor schemes – it cuts down the perceived size of your floor plan – but I went with it as an expensive experiment in determining if the house should be all dark or all white. If you want first-hand advice on which shows up less dirt, I can honestly say it's a dead heat.

Don't assume, though, that the space-defying, light-attracting benefits of white floors come without a price. Here are some tips from those who love and live with white boards:

- Furniture – With white floors, your furniture needs to be up to par. They can be very unforgiving and highlight unsuitable pieces a darker floor would disguise.
- Spatial relations – White floors, especially when combined with coordinated architraves, walls and ceilings, can make the most of small room, giving it a look of seeming endlessness. If you have a large space, though, be sure you have enough stuff to fill it.
- Maintenance – You can have either highly polished, immaculate monastic white floors or slightly distressed, casual floors. The immaculate option needs daily babysitting and sweeping, a shoes-off policy, furniture protectors and a healthy dose of paranoia. The latter is more a duty of care – just accept that there's nothing much you can do about scuffs and marks. Instead, celebrate the character the floor builds through wear and tear.
- Visual impact – Prepare to be dazzled. Living with white floors is like having your glasses cleaned by the optometrist – so sparkling, so clean and fresh.
- Applications – Designer Amanda Mahoney, queen of the white floor, believes that white American oak gives the best boards for lime-washing or staining white. How does she get hers right time after time? Her secret ingredient is a Swedish product called Synteco, an oil to which her contractors add the white. It leaves a matt, raw, natural finish that's very northern hemisphere. If you prefer a flatter, block-white floor, she suggests going for the cheapest boards you can find, since once you've applied the marine or epoxy paint, the only part of the boards you'll see is their width, not their pedigree.
- White-wood boards – No matter if they're the Swedish natural type or the solid, stark variety, floorboards in white wood are possibly the ultimate in pared-back luxury.

Isabella Blow, the late fashion aesthete, preferred white: 'I love white. It just stinks of luxury, I suppose because you have to clean it so often.' While she was speaking of white in terms of fashion, of course, the same applies to white floors. Sure, you have to be fairly conscientious on the cleaning front, but it really does repay you visually.

Original walls

You know how some things you read are so inspiring you cut them out to keep for future reference? Reach for the Post-its, this might be one of them. Some time soon (usually these kinds of days creep up on you – they can't be planned or predicted), you'll realise that you have no prior commitments and the day is yours. You'll look at a bare wall and think, Maybe today's the day. It's been blank for far too long. You know it could do with a dose of something. You've tyre-kicked at galleries but nothing's quite right. The problem is, it doesn't need to be breathtakingly beautiful or indecently expensive, it just needs to be, well, right. You can't see the point in a featureless feature wall (I mean, why paint one wall pea green when the others are white?) and you don't want the television wall-mounted as if it were a wall feature.

Sometimes a room needs a king hit of something that's totally irreverent, completely fun and slightly absurd. The rooms usually in such need are kids' rooms, playrooms, living rooms and informal dining spaces. Overseas magazines have been touting the benefits of wall features for a while now, and the local marketplace has finally caught on. Not only are they value for money, but they're relatively risk-free. If you don't like it two years down the track, move it to another room or take it down with no fear of having wasted too many decorating dollars. Stencils, decals, vinyl artwork, murals, blown-up photography and bespoke commissions all fall into the category of wall features and, considering the size of wall they can take up, can equate to embarrassingly good dollars per square metre.

When you're conceiving an original wall, bear in mind that the room's existing elements will not shine so brightly once it's installed. This is perfect if your room is generally lacklustre in the first place – I mean, it's not like it can get any worse, right? I've seen candid photographs turned into wallpaper (liveprint.com.au), maps that take over the entire room (mapworld.net.au), huge whale-shaped stickers that are secret chalkboards (frenchbazaar. com.au) and Florentine-inspired mirror wall decals (designforuse.com.au). I've seen the simple act of confident stripes painted lengthwise down a wall, and wallpaper that's more decorative than a roll of paper has any right to be (see the Catherine Martin for Porter's Paints wallpaper range – porterspaints.com.au). One of my favourites, though, was based on the simplest of ideas – a whole wall of $40 artist-commissioned tea towels (thirddrawerdown. com) attached with teeny clever Magnart wall magnets (also from thirddrawerdown.com). So good! Sublime in its simplicity and ingeniously savvy.

Whether your ability is limited to applying a sticker or extends to wallpapering or drawing or painting freehand onto the wall, all you've got to lose is a boring room.

Etsy (etsy.com) is a treasure trove of wall art. Take your time and discover bargains, handmade items and unique options. I limit myself to 40 minutes at a time – if I don't, I can be on there the entire night! Ask The Wall Sticker Company (thewallstickercompany. com.au) to make you your very own Tintin – or anything for that matter. The gorgeous Inke Wallpaper Tree is available at Kido Store (kidostore. com), while The Kids Store (thekidsstore.com.au) has more infant-suitable decals. The cutest is Counting On The Wall.

Concrete facts

My eyes get itchy just thinking about worn carpet, so I have a love affair with polished concrete floors that runs hot and cold. One minute I'm saving up to do the entire downstairs in it and the next I'm deliberating over whether it can work with soft furnishings and my compulsion for fabrics. I love the way it can't conceal dust mites and how it looks, in all its transparency, so amazingly clean. But I secretly fear it might be a bit urban. I love its single-minded greyness and how it goes so well with the density of the colour orange (for a high-impact scheme) just as well as powder blue (for greater subtlety). I love the way you can hose it down, which perfectly suits my time-poor, little-care housekeeping routine.

What I didn't really get, though, is why – considering it's such a cheap building material – it's so expensive when you want it for your kitchen floors or benchtops. The simple truth of the matter is labour. It takes a huge amount of work and machinery to tippy-toe into a kitchen and blast level concrete into the confines of a residential floor plan. And then there's its general all-round hotness. When you're the material du jour, you can basically ask any price you like. People who live with it don't ever speak of its price, of course. They talk of their 'investment'. An investment in low maintenance. An investment in eradicating allergies. An investment in devastatingly handsome looks.

We all know more than enough about concrete's maintenance and cleaning advantages, so let's discuss the side not often spoken about – the delicate (but deliberate) ways you can warm it up within an interior. Most of our sophisticated architects have the knack of counterbalancing it texturally. This means that the seating, window dressings and objects they choose are more often than not as pure and weighty in their own right. Whether they're grainy leather, open-weave linens, aged timbers or patina-ed surfaces, they all work to add richness to the purity of the concrete floor.

Stainless-steel legs look great against a concrete floor, but not every wood shade will work, especially not the reddish timbers. Look at your furniture bases and legs, because whatever hits the floor will be more noticeable than usual. And I'm not a fan of placing large, loud, look-at-me rugs over such a beautiful floor. There's more to be gained by working with a subtler palette that sits with the natural beauty of the concrete.

Beyond floors, there are also lovely concrete pieces that take their cues from the modesty the material offers and can add a level of modernity that can't be achieved with woods or veneered pieces. Small items peppered here and there can add an edge to many schemes, both inside and out. While a concrete floor is best paired with furniture constructed from other materials, concrete furniture can be matched to great effect with wood, stone and rugs. Either way, it's a win-win.

Here's a mini guide to keeping concrete floors clean:

- Sealed concrete floors accumulate dirt slowly – They might not look dirty, but when you clean them you'll realise how dirty they were and how much better they look when cleaned.
- Start with sweeping – Then use a dust mop to pick up any fine particles. Give the floor a wet mop with a mild detergent (vinegar and ammonia can damage the finish, so don't be tempted to use either). Lastly, mop with clean warm water to get rid of any soap.
- Maintain the shine – An occasional re-buff is a good idea, and resealing about every three years will protect the floors.

Opposites really do attract

Sometimes a room, for no sound reason, can accidentally 'make' it. You know the ones – you can't quite tell why, but they work and you feel like you fluked it big-time. You try to dissect it, but there's no point – it's a little bit of this thrown in with a little bit of that. If a professional decorator were to present to you the room's elements on a mood board, you'd probably decline it as a concept. But the design cognoscenti know all too well the one secret of these supposed charming little 'accidents'. Its simplicity is blinding and, once you've practised it a couple of times, almost too easy. Here's how it works. You take one element, force it into the same room as something that's its complete opposite and voilà, you have the tension required to pull off opposites.

Here, my friends, is how you can go from a stay-at-home do-it-yourselfer to semi-professional. Designers, of course, do it with aplomb, but the key to their success is (like most things in life) attacking it with *confidence*. If the truth be known, the reason why a decorator, designer or stylist can do it so effortlessly is their third-party status. They can be far more brutal and fierce in marrying things together when they don't have to live with them every day.

Working with opposites can be high on impact and achieved in a short turnaround – unlike some other styles, which can take decades to build up. For immediate effect, consider the following deliberate pairings: high with low, black with white, retro with country, textural with smooth, bright with neutral and, as in the photo, old with new. The beauty of opposites is that they can be plonked together, the tension is created and there you have it.

Opposites are not just about the more visually obvious ends of the spectrum, though. What I love about working with opposites is the more subtle plays. Consider, for example, the quieter interactions between opaque and solid, natural and techno, shiny and matt, high end and low end, and – the most beautiful, sophisticated play of all – oversized with small. Now, this is where decorators demonstrate their flair and prove why they're paid the big bucks where the do-it-yourselfers can fail. The pros know that the ideal is to have one pairing of opposites at work in a room and no more. Don't be the homeowner who, flush with success, practises more than one pairing of opposites. Do one well and leave it alone. The pros also know that the success of opposites is underpinned by their extremes. If your range is only ever so small, the room will tend to tread decorative water.

Here are some unexpected opposites to experiment with:

- French with Japanese.
- Beige with red.
- Floral with concrete.
- Tongue and groove with metal.
- Rough with smooth.
- Shiny with distressed.
- Woven with sleek.

Fresh as a daisy

When it comes to presenting flowers at home, I think it might be best to ignore the lead of the glossy magazines. Flowers are a magazine stylist's best friend, you see. Practically speaking, a huge bunch of peonies, hydrangeas or Ecuadorian roses can disguise a flawed room, and their deliberate placement can cover up any kind of issue within the camera's frame. A dozen floppy tulips can perk up the most lacklustre of mantels, and the teensiest posy of violets can add femininity to an overly masculine room. But doing flowers at home, for real, not just for photography, requires a different approach altogether. It's the chance for little pick-me-ups in unexpected corners of the house, and for exhibits of your favourite blooms.

Here are some foolproof ideas I've garnered from working with the best flowers and florists, as well as from the ever-practical book *Grandiflora Arrangements*, Saskia Havekes' love-letter to DIY flowers:

- When putting a variety of flowers in the one bunch, consider not just their collective colours and shapes but also their scents. While a posy of lilac and tuberose is a potentially beautiful combination, the scents will overpower one another in a small room.
- The $29 Bladet vase from Ikea (ikea.com.au) is great for large arrangements. At 45 centimetres tall, it's also perfect for lilies.
- Resist the urge to fill your vase with water – you only need a little of the stems in water, not half the stem. Cut the stems off and add clean water regularly for maintenance. Spray the heads of hydrangeas to keep them looking fresh.
- Consider coloured ceramics in preference to glass vases; not only do they not show any dirty water, but their colour can set off the flowers. Try a soft green ceramic vessel with red peonies, for example – the contrasting colours are magical.
- Play with the scale of the flowers and the vase. The flowers shouldn't stick as far out of the vase as the vase is high. Shorter vessels work with tall blooms and a taller vase holds shorter stems beautifully.
- Small jam jars and imported drink bottles are charming with a single bud.
- They were once the most over-sent floral thank-you, but phalaenopsis orchids still reign supreme as the ultimate in household flowers.

For more on flowers, see Lisa Cooper's seasonal tips on page 207.

Artful hanging

Choosing what to display on your walls is hard enough, without having another set of dos and don'ts when it comes to hanging them. Art galleries rely on the laws of proportion and spatial relations to achieve maximum impact on their walls. Now hanging your art gallery-style rather than, say, taking a more random, casual approach is just a matter of personal taste, but whatever you want your walls to convey, here is some reliable advice.

Before any nail hits the Gyprock, move the furniture out of the way, lay all of your artworks out on the floor and experiment with them until you find an arrangement you like. Then use the paper-outlines method to find the best arrangement on your wall (see 'Displaying your photographs' on page 116). In my experience, multiple frames look best arranged in a rectangular, square or diamond formation and set in a tight group about 5 centimetres apart. Alternatively, a looser arrangement with some deliberate negative space is the best starting point for a more casual display.

But what if your wall is a work in progress? While I'm waiting (it's a five-year plan!) for my own living-room wall, I've discovered the ingenuity of those 3M hooks that you can move about at whim (luckily I have a penchant for small, exciting works rather than large heavy ones). Every time I buy a new piece, all the others move up and down and around until they look as fabulous as they can while waiting for the 'ideal' set-up. Whether or not that ever happens (highly unlikely, but you have to have something to wish for), there have been some seriously beautiful works in progress.

I've noticed in my house-perving travels that many people often put their 'best' artwork in the master bedroom, which seems a waste of a favourite, given you see it for such a short time at night. I've seen some beautiful paintings hung in the dining room (good for visitors to appreciate) but at a 'walking-by' level, rather than the ideal 'sitting' level. Most of the time you spend in the dining room you're sitting down, so hang your artworks with this angle in mind.

Lighting is often underused when it comes to art, but it can really highlight an artist's work. Generally speaking, when lighting artworks, low-wattage halogens tend to be the most colour-correct. If you're lucky enough to live among sculpture, consider drawing attention to them by training a bulb on them that's three times brighter than the overall light in the room. I once styled a house with an expensive hanging-track system and a sophisticated lighting set-up. The best part about the impressive line-up was seeing their son's Grade 5 lino print lit up with the same reverence as their Renoir.

If the painting you want to hang is large or heavy, it will need at least two hooks – this will also prevent the frame from tilting. Sometimes large paintings can look just as good leaning against a wall. It's best to secure them somehow, but it looks great when the painting's magnificence starts at the floor rather than halfway up the wall. Smug but effective!

All in the fabric

Using fabric successfully in a room (and I don't just mean adding a feature cushion) is a bit like attempting rabbit rillettes as a beginner cook. But some rooms are just meant to be full of soft furnishings and textiles. In the Gramercy Park Hotel in New York (gramercyparkhotel.com) fabrics are just as important as art. Textiles are the one thing most people try to save on, yet in my opinion they're the one element you should really splurge on. One of my fabric heroes, designer Caroline Quartermaine, knows how to get results no matter what your budget. She understands that it's best, and far more sumptuous, to use 'almost any material if in a spirit of generosity'. And she's right.

If you're budget free, by all means buy the very best and loads of it. There's no more beautiful sight than weighty, expensive curtains puddling onto the floor. Fabric can give a room an instant cosy factor, but be forewarned – if overused it can make you feel like you're being choked to death by all that warp and weft. Here are some tips from the top:

- Look at fabrics as an investment – in comfort as well as eye candy. If you choose a fabric you love, you can take it with if you move and it will withstand a variety of home environments from traditional to modern.
- Ensure that the colours within the fabrics are of similar tones but cover a breadth of pattern. In the right room, spots, stripes, patterns and plains will work together if they come from a similar palette.
- The plainer the colour or pattern, the better the fabric quality needs to be, especially if used on a large expanse such as a lounge or curtains.
- Don't let curtain fabric take over the room. If you fall in love with a slightly brave or loud print, consider restricting it to a smaller application, such as a single chair, pelmet or cushion.
- If you're hunting for fabrics, you'll be bombarded with a plethora of options, so decide if you want the fabric for its warmth, colour or interest. This will narrow the field and make your choice less daunting.
- I prefer to let a room flutter with both small and large prints. The smaller detailed fabrics draw you in and the larger formats provide all the wow.
- Use fabrics with gay abandon, especially if your room is a bit of a plain Jane. If your room is impressive architecturally, though, restrain yourself and pull back into simpler, softer applications.

God, I love the term 'puddling', which describes the effect of a curtain length breaking on the floor. You'd use it in context thus: 'I'd like heavy puddling on the dining-room curtains, thank you very much.'

Intermixing with aplomb

The best decorating quote I ever heard came from a friend's mother: 'If you like the things, then they'll all go together because you like them.' In other words, you don't need to worry about anything looking odd or wrong, because they're all in your taste. And this is the basis of today's lesson – well, it's the lovely loophole you can use if it doesn't work out!

Why some people seem to fluke it while others hit the decorative wall has got more to do with self-confidence than anything else. My former florist, Mariella (who sold up and moved to Italy in search of a crumbling seaside villa to buy), was one of those people. Not only could she work serious magic with flowers, but she could also design a feature wall (she did this one) and wrap a birthday gift until it was so incredible-looking it put everyone else's to shame.

Some people, like Mariella, have the gift of intermixing. It's a genetic blessing, just like long legs or the ability to follow maps. Watching her for years taught me a few things I'd like to share with you here:

- Never doubt your visual sense – Having the conviction and courage to actually pull it off is as important as the idea itself.
- When in doubt, go bold – The bolder the better; the pure gutsiness of the idea will pull it through.
- Don't go with the Joneses – Do something different, knowing it will be distinctive no matter what.
- Ignore the rules of what goes with what – Here antique frames sit with the store-bought variety, Chinese artefacts sit atop French, and the rough is paired with the shiny. Once you take the supposed rules out of the equation, you'll have access to far more decorative liberties.
- If you want the unexpected, you need to experiment and play.
- Look to other cultures for inspiration – Due to our country's young age, we're decoratively pretty single-layered. The Moroccans, French, Spanish and Indians have hundreds of years on us, and so they intermix with great deftness.
- Go for a little visual consistency – When working with one defining element, such as a hand-painted wall, select smaller elements within the same colour palette.

Get acquainted with stores and importers that specialise in homewares from specific countries, such as shweshwe.com, rubystar.com, orienthouse.net.au and cambodiahouse.com.au. Intermixed schemes are usually kicked off by one feature piece, and there's a good chance you'll find one at one of these stores. Think of it as saving you a plane trip and the annoyance of shipping the item home. But if you do find yourself making some rash decisions in a market and need to send something home, contact bronel.com. They ship 'personal effects', picking them up from most places and dropping them off at your door.

Make a feature of your wall

This should really be called 'How *not* to do a feature wall'. As far as I'm concerned, there are two types of feature wall. The incorrect type is a single wall of high-energy colour intended to give the living room a bit of pop or spice. I don't believe that one wall should be coloured in an otherwise all-white room. I love it when different shades of the same tone are cleverly used (such as chocolate then a lighter shade of milky latte), but I can't abide one barefaced chocolate wall and three white. No designer would ever do it, because it instantly makes the room look smaller and leads to other design misdemeanours.

The *right* type of feature wall, though, derives its charm and personality from clever object or furniture placement. In every room there's always one wall that just begs for display. Whenever I walk into a house, I mentally move paintings to other walls or swap feature pieces to the other side because, to me, some walls are just gagging for it, while others are simply passive players holding up a ceiling.

Here are some ideas I'd love to have the wall to try:

- Mirrors of all shapes and sizes – They're best either all framed or all unframed. Keep buying them until you have the right mix.
- Teensy artworks – A great way to build up an art collection. (See page 116 for a lesson in hanging them.)
- Jelly moulds – I once hung some of these on metal plate holders down a tongue-and-groove hallway. It was a sight to behold in an otherwise ho-hum passageway devoid of colour.
- Wire cake stands – Peppergreen Antiques owner and one of my decor heroes Carina Cox does this on her own kitchen wall at home. Hail Queen Carina!
- Dog portraits – Or sailor portraits, cat pictures, any specific subject matter.
- Blue items – Or items in any colour you love (blue is just my default colour). If the one constant is a single colour, disparate items will be wall-perfect. Try it with orange, brown, red or cream.
- Twigs and nature – I've seen a wall shelf (Ikea's Förhöja to be exact) supporting a line-up of tiny glass jars filled with sands from various beaches the owners had visited. They'd added a note to each that detailed the date and location.
- Plates – Tried, tested and done to death, but plate displays really do read as art and the sum of their parts is always greater than the whole.
- Book covers – These are art forms unto themselves, so frame your favourites and turn a snoringly boring wall into über eye candy.

The ten best things – and how to own them

Buy well, buy once. It's important to invest in the best version of whatever it is you're after. Here are the top ten things from which I think every home can benefit over time:

1. Lighting – Ingo Maurer's work can cost hundreds of thousands, but my favourite light of his, the Zettle'z 5, is $1700 from Space Furniture (spacefurniture.com.au).
2. Toilet Brush – A luxury or a need? Caroma's Cosmo brush and holder, at only $39 (caroma.com.au), is both, doing the job efficiently without bells or whistles.
3. Glassware – Zafferano's glasses are slightly larger than your standard glass. Their Tumbler 1117 is 100 millimetres high, 95 millimetres in diameter and only $23 at Hub Furniture (see hubfurniture.com.au).
4. Dining chair – Classic bentwood chairs are perfect in walnut, red or white. I love them with natural beech sox on the legs – $215 from Thonet (thonet.com.au).
5. Feature seat – Sometimes a full-blown hero lounge is too much, but Gervasoni's Ghost 09 Love-seat is the bomb. It's fit for two, and its baggy linen dress just begs to be sat on – $2895 from Anibou (anibou.com.au).
6. Garbage bin – I've never managed to get a grown-up hidden-away version, but I'm more than content with the Cookie Monster-style Knodd bin (with pedal-operated lid action) – $35 from Ikea (ikea.com.au).
7. Bedware – Sleep in what you like is what I say. I have my own bed-linen brands that I love and covet and save up for, but *the* dressing gown *everyone* should own is less than $100 from Acland Home (acland.co.nz).
8. Butcher tiles – You can't get simpler than when these are laid brickwork-style, and you really can't tell if they're über-expensive or little cheapies. About $22 per square metre for 10 × 20 centimetre tiles from Academy Tiles (academytiles.com.au).
9. Art – Good galleries welcome all-comers and all questions, and love talking about their favourite topic. Art bought with your heart will never disappoint, despite the ups and downs of the market. How about the uplifting cloud portraits (from $3500) by fine art photographer Trevor Mein (meinphoto.com)?
10. Candles – I'm generally opposed to the 'expensive candle' category, but I do make an exception for Cire Trudon. The blueblood of candles, they burn for 70 hours, sit in brown mouth-blown glasses and are basically without peer – $95 from Becker Minty (beckerminty.com).

Living in black and white

They're not even officially colours, but black and white are perfect partners. These perpetual pick-me-ups can perform some impressive decorative stunts when they're allowed to get together. Take, for example, the way they can make middle-of-the-road pieces look decidedly dramatic and defy their price tags or provenance. (For more on this point, see 'Creating drama in black and white' on page 106.) The sheer simplicity of black and white can stop you in your tracks (although the zebra crossing probably has a lot to do with this). And what about the way that black with white can work to point out the finer details within a room?

But where do you start? Should there be more *noir* than *blanc*? Well, unless you like the hypnotic effects of Pop Art, it's best to apply my three-to-one rule: that is, use three times the amount of black or white compared with the other. Trust me, it's devastatingly impressive when you use three parts white to one part black (and works really well for white in combination with other shades too).

How do you go about placing all your coloured objects, vases and artwork in between all the black and white? The good news is that three parts black to one part white will look amazing with a hint of colour. In fact, anything you put against it instantly looks more expensive, more covetable – and harder to find. This is great news for struggling decorators or those with a minimalist bent, because it means you need less stuff, generally speaking. A dash of colour is the key to black and white's mystery – and red, aubergine and metallics are black and white's latest best friends. Use sophisticated autumnal colours and metallic tones in rich textures to add a beautiful layer to your room. Or you could stick with adding just a bright splice of red to punctuate the space.

So how do you get started? It's safe to say that if you've ever had success painting a wall white, you'll do even better with black. If white is the exposer of truths (bad rendering, cracking cornices, uneven ceiling heights), black is the ultimate disguise. It can make just about anything look great (ask any woman who owns an LBD). The key to nailing the right black and not having a living room that looks like a day club is to step back a bit from real black and try a dark grey instead. This handsome shade has the same intensity and still lets anything white smash right up against it, but won't make the room feel like it's in mourning.

Sure, it's not a scheme for every room in the house, but it can definitely do wonders for a lacklustre space. It won't cost you any more than going down the white-on-white route, but it will give you so much more back.

For some stunning black and white paints, try Bauwerk's (bauwerk.com. au) 14/55 and 18/80. The latter is a soft black, more shale than *noir*, and is gorgeously handsome with wooden furniture.

Colour your world

Although blue is my all-time favourite, there's really not a colour I don't like. Even that manila-folder beige can look dynamite alongside a regal blue, a dark grey or an orange. No famous decorator, past or present, has reached icon status without using colour to their advantage. There are lots of textbook, tried-and-true combinations, but I love it when styling assignments take me to houses that offer living proof that a supposed colour no-no really can work. Ignore the old 'Blue (or red) and green should never be seen without a colour in between' untruth. Or the decree that pink and red should be kept separate at all times. There are no rules when it comes to colour.

Nothing warms a room more than colour, whether it's used as a unified statement or in an unexpected bolt. Katrina Hill, a decorator of high repute and a user and abuser of colour, shares my view that colour is just as important in the home as air. Katrina, though, being the designer in demand that she is, can get away with much more raucous applications than, say, you or I. She's even gone so far as to ask her cabinetmaker to line her cutlery drawers with orange felt (which, by the way, looks great)!

But of all the advice I've gleaned from Katrina over the years, the one piece that has stuck in my mind and rings most true is to apply colour appropriateness. By that she means that the colour needs to be suited to the environment, the application, the climate and the user: 'Use stimulating colours in the places you're up and about in and put subtle colours to work when you want to relax.' She advises, for example, against painting a child's room red, otherwise you run the risk of them becoming overstimulated in the room they're meant to be sleeping in. And, she says, there's no point using green in a room that overlooks the garden. Before you go out and apply your all-time favourite colour as a complete room option, think again. Katrina suggests we consider the all-important *context* of the colour. The colour of your sandstone bricks can look fab in your bricks, but match the colour with paint and it can look all wrong, taking on a flatness it never had in the bricks. Instead, select bite-sized (and less risky) elements that will add some energy and colour to an almost neutral room.

The experts suggest running with a courageous combination you'd never be game to try anywhere else by employing what the trade calls the 'extremities'. By this they mean rugs, artwork, objects, cushions, glassware and side lighting – the smaller brushstrokes – which can be played with and practised. This is the simplest way, for example, to test out the satisfying results of combining pink and red.

Sing the blues

I'm mad about blue. Matisse blue. Klein blue. Raj blue. Navy blue. Powder blue (fab with strawberry red à la Cath Kidston or drop-dead gorgeous with chocolate brown). I'm absolutely nuts about it. I go into a shop and only see the blue option. My eBay searches all end in backslash blue.

But apart from my personal cravings for it, I believe blue to be the one colour that goes the extra mile in a professional decorating sense. Let's see . . . You can put it against birch wood and it comes over all Scandi, neat and clean. Place it against handsome dark woods and it takes on a regal air. Use it with antiques and it can remove that stuffiness. But see what happens when it's added to white (as here)! Grab your shades – it's dynamic, fresh and contemporary.

Blue is the workhorse of the colour palette, the ultimate multi-tasker, working with anything you throw at it. It's been the muse of many an artist, and in the work of, say, Yves Klein or Matisse, there's good evidence of its effect. The trick with blue, I believe, is to take your cue from the artists but use it sparingly – yet deliberately. Its most natural pairing (and most popular colour combination according to Dulux sales records) is with sunny yellow – echoing the sand and the sea.

According to colour theory, blue is restorative and relaxing, which makes it perfect for bedrooms and sitting rooms. A friend has recently done the splashbacks for her black-and-white kitchen in turquoise-blue larger format tiles – with stunning results. I'd try, though, to avoid blue in bathrooms, where it seems far too literal a choice. It's also best avoided in rooms that host spectacular ocean views: if you're lucky enough to see water from the room, it's best not to mimic it – it will never be as beautiful as the real deal.

Light blues befriend red and chocolate, mid blues love mid greens and ivory, and dark blues are perfect with woody tones, orange and celery green. At the height of my blue phase, I painted my bedroom bright blue. I kept it for a year and it had the same effect as a gin and tonic. While it can eventually become boring in a confined place such as a bedroom, that year I really did have the most sleep I'd ever had.

If I were a colour I'd be blue. What colour are you? Get yourself colour-coded at mycolormyidea.com – it's really fun! Another fun site is colorstrology.com: it gives a colour depending on the month and a shade depending on the date. Being September-born, I couldn't be happier with my blue colour allocation.

All white now

White is more complex than it seems. It's the world's preferred neutral and every renovator's best friend – that is until they get tripped up by it. Architects master it, but they've studied for years. Homeowners see it as a one-colour-suits-all solution, and herein lies the double-edged decorative sword: lulled into a false sense of security, you begin to think that all whites are first cousins, but nothing could be further from the truth.

White is the hardest shade of all to get right – a real chameleon under different lights and in different situations – which is why it's hard, almost irresponsible, to say one white is superior to another without seeing them in situ. For some, Dulux's White Watsonia (dulux.com.au) is the standby, but use this in a room with a different orientation and you'd swear the mixer at the paint shop had made a mistake.

A room's contents can also affect how your white behaves. Large dark pieces of furniture will give it a sombre feel, just as over-bright feature lighting can transform a wall under its glow. These issues aside, white can work as the ultimate highlighter, showing off a space at its best – which is why a white-on-white room can be so intoxicating. Art gallery walls are a case in point, rarely straying from white – they act as silent brokers to a sale by highlighting a painting's best features. In the same way that white enhances a room's best features, it will also highlight its worst: imperfect plastering, uneven rooflines and the like are all magnified when a room is painted white.

In my experience, slightly off-white shades will add the desired brilliance but are a little more discreet. Think almost-open white tulips, ivory tableware, slipper chairs upholstered in *blanc*, all under a glassy chandelier. And if you want to add a dash of colour, then turn to 'Working colours into white' on page 154.

Which white paint is best for your walls? Some favourite whites I've prised from architect friends are Dulux's Antique White USA (dulux.com. au), Murobond's Powder (murobond.com.au), Resene's Laminex Cararra and Rice Cake (resene.com.au), and Wattyl's MCA Gallery White (wattyl. com.au). I pass these on with all care and no responsibility. Best get a sample pot of each and test them at home yourself.

In the red

It's sometimes sexy, sometimes scary, but there's something persistently courageous and fabulous about working with red. Take it down the brown scale and it's all grown up, full of confidence and sophistication. Keep it cherry-like and it's glorious, familiar and childlike. I find red a great device if a room has little or no redeeming features. In the same way a swipe of red lipstick can really improve a ho-hum outfit, a dash of red can give a standard room something to hang onto.

If a room, for example, has an unsightly view, red is a sure-fire way of keeping all the attention within the floor plan. It also makes any object seem supersized: one red lounge really looks one and a half times as big as a non-red lounge, and if a red lampshade were put beside a white one, you'd swear it was larger in diameter. This says a lot about red's ability to blind a room with its boldness, distracting from the minor details and imperfections in its way.

Only the bold go with red as a hero colour – and are rewarded handsomely with cheers and applause from their neutral-loving friends. Others are smug in the knowledge that red is a little helper, pepping up beige, latte and other neutrals. It's stunning with a black-and-white scheme. It's heavenly (in its true strong-red form) with soft apple green or powder blue. It's truly fresh when mixed one part red to one part white. And if it's partnered in prints with pink and orange, the room really needs nothing else.

One scheme that's often overlooked, though, is red with brown, black and orange. Smart and handsome as it comes, it's the perfect antidote to modern contemporary furniture styles. If you're stuck for a reliable guide as to how much colour you should include in one scheme, a really good place to start is Taubman's 603010 rule. The theory is, you deem one colour to be your main tone (at sixty per cent), then use two highlight colours in proportions of thirty per cent and ten per cent – which puts you in line for 100 per cent success! The 603010 rule won't be the answer to all colour combinations every time, but it will lead to some very happy marriages, and works perfectly with the little firebomb that is red!

Red glass is a beautiful thing to collect, and a fail-safe way to use red sparingly. It gives a smack of colour, but since it's glass you can move it if you want to. I look for mine at bric-a-brac stores, on eBay and in gift and homeware shops like House or Bed Bath N' Table. It's amazing how an el-cheapo vase in the right red can look so much more expensive than the same one in, say, orange or pink.

Working colours into white

Seemingly the easiest thing in the world to do, right? You have an all-white space, you simply add a splash of colour here and there and bingo! Well, not exactly. This is where many decorating efforts can fall shy of magnifique. White can look all easy-peasy, but it's the trickiest beast there is.

When working with white, don't underestimate its magical powers. Its popularity is completely misleading – it's not the safest colour to do and is by no means the most foolproof. In actual fact, it should come with a ten-point warning. White is the ultimate game-player and master of disguise. It can expose everything that's wrong about a room or show up the smallest of flaws.

People often find that when they bring their new cushion, rug, lounge or curtain home it looks completely different from how it looked in the showroom or store. People even go so far as to swear they've taken home the wrong one, but it's just that the lighting, wall colour and environment in a retail situation are so very different from those in a residential one. Houses usually have more natural light sources and, even if you had the same Dulux Stowe White on your walls as they did in the store, your windows, ceiling height and flooring can have a huge impact on the end result. When making big decorating decisions, it's reasonable to take a sample of your paintwork with you. Bristol Paints (bristol.com.au) now do very handy A3 bumper swatches.

Here are some things to bear in mind if you're adding colour to your white room:

- Think it through – Consider the effect of your coloured pieces within the context of the white room in which they'll sit. A blue-based white can make blue upholstery look grey, while a stark white can make a medium pink look like a screaming one.
- Stay flexible – Introducing, say, an olive-green ottoman to this room would take it somewhere else entirely. This is a great starting point for rooms you need to save up for as you go and need to add to constantly. It becomes a room that never sits still, and that can be pretty exciting.
- Go for personality – Colour really is the mainstay of successful decorating; without it, rooms risk being void of any real personality. Not to try is worse than trying and getting it wrong. The power of colour can be nothing short of incredible.

Colour can save furniture. A cheap piece can look even cheaper upholstered in a neutral shade, because it reveals flaws, dubious finishes or telltale signs of lower quality craftsmanship, but the same piece in a mad colour makes these blemishes harder to decipher.

The colour purple

Purple is an *it* colour. Just like the *it* bag or the *it* hairstyle, it reigns supreme. In its duality it adds opulence to modern rooms and neo-Victorian lushness to traditional ones. It was the *it* colour of last year's Milan Furniture Fair and, because it's a combination of the warmest (red) and coolest (blue) colours, it's a favourite of artists.

Although my favourite colour is blue, I do love purple second best. What I love about working with purples and all the shades of plum and lilac in between is how it's a soft–hard colour. Although it's a powerful hue, representing wealth, power, reverence and royalty, it can be the softening agent in an exceptionally stark or hard room. It's also the colour to encourage artistic endeavours.

Whenever someone wants a black lounge or major piece, I suggest we try a purpley version instead. Eight times out of ten this works – purple adds a magical softness to most room schemes. While it doesn't ever replace black, it gives so much more.

Ready to embrace the colour of kings? Try these simple suggestions:

- Never use purple as the hero, all-consuming colour – It's far too complex for that. Use it instead in single pieces, such as a lounge (as here), armoire, feature light shade or bed head. My ideal? Upholstered on a swan chair in the corner of a room.
- Dip your toes in the water first – Hunt for purple-based accessories that you can place in a room to see how it works. Purple is equally at home in a polychromatic scheme and a neutral or all-white one.
- Let it come through in your fabrics – Botanical prints, with their green inclusions, contrast sensationally with purple.
- Stick to one version of it – Unlike shades of red or black, purples can't be used together in their numerous gradations towards white. Pick one shade and love it.
- Avoid using it near windows framing bright blue seas or the beach – Add purple only when the room has no strong vantage points. It keeps the eye inside and entertains it there.
- Consider how gorgeous it looks against concrete surfaces – It's the ultimate colour (even better than blue) for warming up concreted spaces.
- Match it with pure whites, creamy ivories and grey with confidence.
- Accept that some things in life were never meant to be purple – For example, all four walls of a living room or exterior brickwork.

Here are some things that are just great in purple:

- Window dressings – Consider neutral curtains with lilac bottom tabs. Yum!
- Glassware on a windowsill.
- A flat top sheet folded over on an all-white bed. Hello, freshness!

getting down to
brass tacks

You *can* have tidy kids

God bless our little children, but who'd have thought that such little beings could create so much mess? Decking out your child's room (especially your first-born's) can be a bit like arranging a wedding – once you're in the zone, you can no longer hear sense or take words from the wise. While I'm not an expert on the subject of living stylishly with children, I do know that they never grow out of their messiness (I'm told it just becomes a different kind of mess) and that their rooms never do get any bigger (have you ever heard of renovation money being used to increase the kids' quarters rather than for a new kitchen?).

When furnishing a child's room, try to resist the cutesy charms of infant furniture and think of your offspring's longer term needs. You should also sidestep any complete look – such as matching wall friezes, bed heads and curtains – which is sure to date. Ask yourself if the main furniture and decorative elements will still look good when he or she reaches Grade 1. Doing a bedroom up every five years just doesn't make decorative sense, given there are so many other new things to buy and fabulous ideas to consider for the needier rooms of the house. You should also relinquish any idea that children have reasonable storage requirements. Those store-bought kids' wardrobes might look cute, but they'd be hard pushed to accommodate any five-year-old's winter and summer school uniforms, let alone their full regalia. If budget and space allow, install the tallest, widest built-ins you can manage. Until then, you'll need to perform some crafty space-defying, storage-solving acts.

If you're living at maximum capacity with no more cupboard space, here's one tip I've found successful (be warned, though, it takes discipline and extreme willpower and you will risk being labelled a right hypocrite). Only let your kids get something new if they throw out something old – it's a simple case of numbers: one thing in = one thing out. No child ever goes with the 'Okay, I'll keep the one I have at home' option, but this system means that you keep on top of things, rather than have to endure those teary annual clean-outs that always seem to happen on the last day of the holidays.

In the interim, there are some fabulous child- and style-friendly storage options out there that will grow as your little darlings do (check out equatorhomewares.com.au and hsw.com.au, for example). Like most things in the decorative world, with kids' furniture you usually get what you pay for, but whether you spend a little or a lot, you *can* retrieve some sense of order.

Kids' items generally have a one-to-three-year lifespan, so why keep it for ten, just in case? Trade your kids' things at kidspot.com.au. Otherwise, log onto babykidsmarket.com.au and see when an age-specific market day is happening near you. Do you really need to hang onto that three-wheeler pram? Sell it, take the money and go buy yourself a potted orchid. That's much better!

How to do a kid's desk

While we busy ourselves packing living rooms into dining spaces and playrooms into sitting rooms, a separate kids' study is, for most of us, a thing of the past. This has probably got a lot to do with the rise and rise of the 'investment dining table' – the main dining table in most houses is usually a one-stop shop for doing homework, completing tax returns and eating steak tartar (often all in the one shift). And while it's a well-known fact that books have been written on boats and park benches or during commutes, the majority of them have been crafted thanks to the discipline of the desk.

Whether your kids actually *need* a specially assigned desk is completely up to you, but if you do have a corner available, it's got to be better than setting up another TV area. The best thing about a desk is that it can multitask: your kids will transform it swiftly into a fruit and veg shop, a beauty parlour or a construction site for Lego. Pull it away from the wall and they'll become a bank-teller or company manager.

Here are some things to consider when setting up a desk for the kids:

- Let them have a say in the desk and its contents – They're more likely to be interested if given the responsibility of such an important decision.
- Once you've bought the desk, maintain their interest in it, its uses and its contents – Let them decorate, manage and dress it however they want. It can be the one space in the room or house that is their exclusive domain. You can also sustain their enthusiasm by buying some of the fun, small-change desk accessories available in such shops as Smiggle (smiggle.com.au) or kikki.K (kikki-k.com.au).
- Don't insist that it be an über-efficient work spot – The whole idea is for them to have a refuge that they can manage however they please (within reason, of course).
- Choose a unit with a reasonable amount of storage but not too much – The more drawers and nooks you have, the more inevitable it is that they will become stuffed with rubbish, so a one- to three-drawer unit will usually provide enough storage space without becoming too unmanageable.
- Resist (if you can) their desire for a computer – If they must have one, make sure the desk has enough depth for the monitor to be placed as far back as possible.
- If space is really at a premium in their room, sacrifice the bedside table or another relatively superfluous piece of furniture in favour of a desk. You never know what you might be starting.

Love your books

Some say books are destined for the same fate as Beta tapes and LPs, but anyone who's had to endure reading a piece of gripping writing on a computer screen knows that books will never go away. In my travels as an interiors stylist, I've enjoyed visits to many a magnificent pile, and one thing I've noticed is, the bigger the house the smaller the bookcase. Now I know this is a generalisation of the highest order, and it doesn't mean that people with trophy houses don't read. One of the delicious things about being loaded (I wouldn't know myself) must be being able to buy every book ever written about your favourite subject or by your favourite author; another would be putting bespoke library outfitters Groth & Sons on speed-dial.

I'm convinced that books can really make a house a home. Not only can they take you to places you've never been before, but they add a decorative element, almost a well-thumbed look, to any room or house – just ask anyone who collects Penguin Classics. Unlike music, which is usually plastic-wrapped and best hidden away, books add an inimitable element of colour and design to the most mundane of shelves. And you can squeeze a book-storage area into even the smallest of spaces. I recently came across an ingenuous DIY bookshelf – made from Besser-brick side supports and cut-pine shelving for less than $50 – holding the centre of one man's universe: more than 500 books. Thrifty nifty! On the other hand, I have seen the impressive New York floor-to-ceiling custom-made loft library pictured here. The owner, a dedicated reader, aims to fill the shelves only with books she's completely devoured, which means she's still got plenty of great books to look forward to.

Sometimes the best ideas are more about ingenuity than money, and between these polar opposites there's plenty of scope for booklovers, from wall-hung Bookworm shelves that instantly add literary sculpture to any room, to antique cabinets with glass doors that act as giant dust jackets for your favourites. An empty, unused fireplace is ideal for large volumes, which you can stack in a creative way within the confines of the cube. A shelf above any doorway – with bookends to prevent any dangerous spillage – is another space-saving option. You can instantly transform a dining room into a library by adding just one wall of well-placed cabinetry. And what about the gorgeously handsome Ptolomeo 'Tower of Knowledge' book tower (see spacefurniture.com – hit the link to Moco). This tower of strength can give up to 100 volumes a sense of priority and order.

When planning your library space, bear in mind that you should avoid placing your books in direct sunlight – they'll fade in the long run. Save your favourite hardbacks from dust and scuffing by wrapping them in plastic. (Please don't wrap this one, though, unless it's a gift – I want it to be well thumbed!)

The best thing about being a booklover is that you can indulge your passion anywhere in the world. At home, I love to visit any Elizabeth's Bookshop (elizabethsbookshop.com. au) and the Berkelouw Book Barn in the Southern Highlands (berkelouw.com. au/about/berrima) for a real first-edition treat. See page 207 for my favourite bookshops in the world.

Finding (and funding) your collection

Let me introduce you to a word: *oniomania*, Greek for the uncontrollable desire to buy things. Some of us also have keepomania, but here's a radical thought: you don't have to keep everything you buy! That is, of course, unless you're a Collector. Collecting seems like good clean wholesome fun until you realise it's taken up your entire weekend, filled your home to the rafters, made you dizzy with excitement and rendered you penniless. Some people inherit the collecting gene, others seek it out. Some (okay, me) treat it like an incurable disease and just learn to live with it – or, rather, let the dealers deal with them and lure them into irresistible purchases.

The marvellous thing about collecting is you can do it whatever your budget. I've seen incredible collections of hair combs, dice, cake-cooling stands, love letters from the 1940s and other humble, bare-basic things that can be secured for small change. I've also seen museum-worthy collections of Lalique crystal, French rolling pins and snuff bottles. All of these collections, regardless of their market value, have one thing in common: at some point or another they have made the heart of their owner skip a beat.

Collecting means that anywhere you travel, you hope to find more of what you collect, and that you make your chosen fetish your favourite search on eBay. Basically, people will collect anything. Mao and More's John Williams says he does a swift trade in Tibetan human skulls and hip-bone flutes, while Lawson Menzies recently sold a Fireball pinball machine to a collector for almost $5000.

When it comes to starting a collection, there are no rules – apart, perhaps, from always following your heart and buying what you like. With the current global economic meltdown, there's no such thing as a sure bet, so collecting purely for investment reasons could be dicey. Of course, there are items that will always hold their worth, and others (think Gwyn Hanssen Pigott ceramics, Murano glass, Clement Meadmore bronzes) that would be insanely satisfying to collect. But people usually start a collection for more emotional reasons and, because of that, they are rarely ever finished: if you love Spode, you'll always find room for one more piece.

Unless your home has the architectural poetry of Mies Van der Rohe's Farnsworth House, a collection can add a much-needed injection of character into a soulless space suffering from a catalogue-showroom fit-out. I put aside a little each month to feed my fetishes: haberdashery, Dutch portraits and glassware. That way my expenditure can never be questioned. I even have a title for these small contributions in my budget spreadsheet: 'Happy Tax'. And that's exactly what it is.

If there's an obsession, there's group therapy or a website for it. Some of my favourite specialist sites are:

- thebuttonbower.com
- onlineantiques.com.au
- carters.com.au
- mybower.com.au
- maoandmore.com
- rubylane.com
- izziandpopo.com.au
- mitchellroadauctions.com
- circa-c20.com.au
- chinafinders.com.au
- mjshells.com.au

Working with antiques

Once a trend like minimalism sweeps over, the natural urge is to go completely in the opposite direction. Antiques go a long way to filling the void left by minimalism. I once styled the home of Adrian, an antiques dealer, for a magazine shoot, and what he'd done had me in raptures. He'd taken the pedigreed air of pre-loved antiques and placed them in a family-friendly space with much decorating aplomb. Upon closer inspection, I realised what it was that made his rooms so warm yet so established. Most of his pieces were random items, not quite perfect enough in the eyes of his picky clientele, but fine for him, arranged as they were in a fairly haphazard fashion.

Most of the time, antiques can take on a really sombre, heavy look. What Adrian had done so masterfully was lighten them up by painting his rooms in *real* colours rather than safe neutrals. Rich yellow (think a dulled sunflower petal), brilliant blue and cheerful red (rather than antique red) became the modern backdrop for these pieces that had seen decades of decorative styles.

Designers are constantly referring to the past – sometimes to create a shock factor by presenting the old in a new way, but usually because it takes us back to former times and allows us to wallow comfortably in nostalgia. Antiques – when kept well – really pay for themselves. A case in point is the Chesterfields, which reward you the longer you keep them. There's nothing quite so useful as a wooden-topped dining table where you can entertain a dozen friends *or* do your tax return.

Here are some things to consider when working with antiques:

- Remember that, in the right room, old can really reveal a sexy young skin. For real impact, use an old hero piece in a newer, more contemporary room, or a modern piece within an established environment.
- Use glass objects and ornaments to break up heavy bookcases and units.
- Introduce colour by painting the walls, leaving the antiques to provide naturally dark accents. If you'd rather stay with neutrals on your walls, antiques are usually best against a creamy white rather than a stark gallery white.
- And if your budget or time doesn't permit you to source authentic antiques, there's a plethora of new pieces available that pay fairly good tribute to the real thing.

If you love old, you'll adore thedrillhall.com.au, a treasure trove in New Norfolk, Tasmania, set up by a pair of sisters (who married a pair of brothers!). They have an impressive collection of perfect pieces that would sit so beautifully with the new. Their prices are impressive too. Possibly one of Tasmania's best attractions.

Resourcefulness is next to joyousness

A friend recently gave me a teapot with a crocheted cover. It was a lovely random gift that wasn't for a birthday or a special occasion, so it really did take me by surprise. It's not the usual old nana-style tea cosy, either. No, this one should win a crochet award or something. The woman who made it must have an innate sense of colour. It's not the sort of concoction you usually see in op shops, with standard cheap wool colours mashed together any old how, but a wonderful cacophony of reds, blues, greens and black with a touch of yellow as an extra embroidered detail. What was she thinking when she made this, I wonder. I bet it wasn't, 'I'm going to make the most amazing tea cosy the world has ever seen.' She was just going about her crocheting business, happily making something useful.

My friend, who is sick of me thanking her for it, saw it at St Vinnies and thought I would like it for my props room. Stuff the props room, I'm using it every day in her honour and I don't even drink tea – I just make everyone else drink it. I've even started asking casual acquaintances over for tea so I can get maximum use from it. Three dollars can give a lot of joy, but then so can $3000 – the difference lies in how you use it.

Here are my favourite places for playing 'resourceful':

- vinnies.org.au – A gracious way to express our social conscience, giving and buying to support those who have no choice but to be really resourceful.
- hfoc.com.au – Home Furniture on Consignment, read savings, savings, savings.
- 506070.com.au – The form and colour for which the 1950s, 1960s and 1970s are renowned are represented here under the expert eye of Mike Dawborn.
- thesocietyinc.com.au – Check in often, as stylist Sibella Court's purchasable curations change four times a year.
- izziandpopo.com.au – Register your interest or buy straightaway and be notified when your desirables land in Melbourne. *Très* good.
- amorylocura.com – For the inherent charm Argentinean antiques seem to have been given as a birthright.
- davidmetnicole.com – He's English, she's Australian, and together they've brought us Brit chic.
- elements.net.au – Look here for large, character-filled antiques.
- salvage.com.au – Devastatingly handsome recycled flooring along with charming timber pieces.
- thecountrytrader.com.au – Absolute porn for the decorator.

Stealing space

There's a convincing theory that the rise and rise of the bathroom is due to the fact that it's seen as the last bastion of the single-use space. It's the one room where it's almost impossible to multitask – its only prerequisites are to provide facilities for washing, cleaning and relaxing. The same cannot be said for the living room or the kitchen, both now multifunctional centres for entertaining, meal preparation, relaxation, homework, tax returns, counselling sessions, tea-drinking and Scrabble. Sometimes these rooms perform up to five different roles simultaneously.

And this is why it's useful – no matter where or how you live – to conduct an annual house audit. Don your space-efficient hat and look around. Could the landing become a homework station? Could the entry stand in as an impromptu family art gallery? Can the space between the master bedroom and the bathroom play host to a music area? Rather than look at your home in terms of its decorative aspects, scrutinise its floor plan in order to uncover its spatial possibilities.

Sometimes you need an objective stranger to bring your home's spatial potential to your attention. Making every piece of space account for itself is a lesson in knowing what your needs are and then finding the right solutions. These could be: a desk that at first glance looks like a cupboard but opens out to form a fully fledged office; a behind-the-door hanging device that can double your bathroom storage; or under-bed drawers, such as Ikea's ever-so-clever queen-sized Sultan Arno mattress base with storage at $500 (ikea.com.au) for packing away your out-of-season clothes.

Small spaces can sometimes suffer from clutter overload. One simple solution can be to allocate areas for each particular sort of clutter, rather than having it stretch over every surface in the house. Whereas a small arrangement over one mantelpiece can be striking or a small wall filled with art or pictures can add visual impact, both of these simple ideas would be too much if they were applied to every surface or wall in the house.

A space audit can pay handsome dividends. I had a personal win during my last audit when I removed the internal shelving from a hopeless linen cupboard – fortunately I had another linen press closer to the laundry, so I put all my linen in there. Simply by adding a new ledge at desk height and installing power, I turned the previously useless space into a work station. The ledge is shallower than the cupboard, so when the office chair is pushed in and the door closed, the contents are perfectly concealed.

When conducting your own space audit, first run your tape measure over hallways, landings, impractical linen presses or other built-in storage cavities, and those aimless voids some houses seem to have. Just leave the bathroom well alone – it's sacred territory.

Here are some dinky space stealers you need to know about:

- Magazine holders in white from kikki.K (kikki-k.com.au).
- A4 Flat Single Drawer from Howards Storage World (hsw.com.au).
- Wave Mobile Phone Holder from Georg Jensen (georgjensenstore.com.au).

Rearranging your furniture

My house is in a state of constant impermanence. Don't get me wrong, I love my house (or at least I love what it will become one day), but it's just too costly to renovate right this very second. This means I'm always saying things like, 'Why bother doing that up now? It'll only need redoing when the roof comes off anyway,' and other broad statements that do nothing but prolong the house's stalemate. So I'm continually concocting ways to make this in-between state seem a little more bearable.

When, in my job as a stylist, we're shooting other people's homes for magazines, we will sometimes move larger pieces of furniture around to get a better photo. More often than not, the owners, in love with the new set-up, insist we leave things in their new positions once the shoot is over. Sometimes, all you need is an outside opinion, because it's virtually impossible to be subjective about a room you see every day.

And so, when I found myself with no real plans one rainy long weekend when no shops were open, facing a day at home alone in a house that isn't very homey, I put my theory to the test. I was dumbfounded by the immediate results: I moved my bed so that it now looks straight across to the French windows (Why wasn't it there all along? I asked myself). This means that the superfine legs of my bedside tables can now be appreciated when you walk into the room, instead of being hidden by the bed.

The 'when in doubt, move it about' theory costs nothing. Try these five tricks and don't tell me it's not better:

1. Adjust your lounge chairs so that the elements are 'talking' to one another. This could mean moving them away from the walls. You're aiming for a nice place to nestle – a conversation-pit.
2. Assign one piece of furniture or artwork to act as the focal point. Draw attention to it by altering its position to a breakaway spot in the room.
3. Take that doona cover off now and replace it with a fresh new one. While you're at it, play opposites with the bed. It might be in the best position now, but it can't hurt to double check.
4. Reposition the television so that it's not the first thing you see when you enter the room.
5. Keep moving things around. Studies show that cockroaches are more likely to frequent areas where they detect low movement – another perfectly sound reason to keep things on the move.

Living large

When you have a huge room you fill it with huge things, right? Right on! Scale is best appreciated when the size of the room is matched by the size of the decorative elements within it. Take, for example, the huge drawing rooms of the eighteenth century: they were a sensational size, but they were let down by the fact that everything within them drew the eye to their individual intricacies rather than letting the pure grandeur of the room take over. Once we as designers and homeowners understand this problem, we can merge the old and the new to stunning effect.

Take a room with the ceiling height and overall proportions of an eighteenth-century ballroom, replace the old-style buffet with a floating credenza and modern artwork, and you have heaven on a stick. In my opinion, large-scale elements make an impressively sized room look even more impressive. All you need to do is hold back a little more than you usually would, to give more than enough breathing room to each piece. This technique will also make each item seem far more expensive and beautiful than it really is.

If you're fortunate enough to have a big room to fill, go easy on the fit-out. Here are some tips from someone who's really a large-scale person trapped in a small-scale dwelling:

- Try fabrics and colour ways in textured neutrals. They offer a beautiful restraint and will rarely let you down.
- Try to avoid fabrics with oversized (or any size!) patterns. They will shrink even a large room within seconds – it will be like 'Bang! Where did my room go?'.
- Consider three- and four-seater lounge suites with a breakaway configuration to give yourself some flexibility in the composition of the seating.
- Try softer fabrics on your lounges, such as suedes, wool, cotton and linen. Large expanses of leather can make a space look scarily like a showroom.
- To avoid that showroom look, buy up big on ceramics and decorative objects that show off your personal taste. There's nothing sadder than full floor-to-ceiling shelving with not enough in it.
- Select light fittings that are decorative pieces as well as light sources. Large rooms can handle the imposing stature of a full-sized standard lamp.
- Include some decorative elements that will soften up the room, such as blankets, throws and rugs in harmonising tones.
- Consider the Jasper couch from King Furniture (kingfurniture.com.au), the Lunar Pendant from Tub Design (email James at tubdesign@ihug.com.au) or the Applique rug by bernabeifreeman from Designer Rugs (designerrugs.com.au).

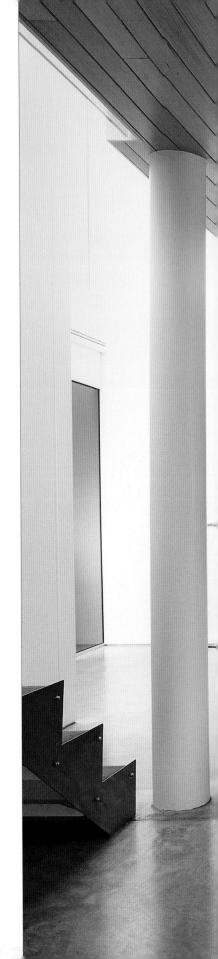

Accommodating that TV

In my opinion, televisions have taken the 'living' out of living rooms. Decoratively speaking, they are space-hoggers, dominating wall and often floor space that could be used for furniture or art. And however bad one television might be, it's not uncommon for me to see as many as four sets in the one semi (that's Sydney for half-a-house). But given TVs are the main element in almost every living room, what truly surprises me is that they come in only one screen colour (piano black) and three casing colours (silver, black, white or combinations of these). Considering that the majority of households err towards neutral schemes, TVs are, visually speaking, crude necessities that we just have to work around.

Why is it, though, that while everything else seems to get smaller, televisions just get bigger and bigger? Technology merchant Len Wallis Audio sells a Panasonic that is 103 inches long (that's 2.2 metres!) for just under $70 000. Whereas 42 inches used to be the norm, the average is now creeping up to a 70 inch screen. I mean that's the width of a Barina! Imagine parking that in your living room sideways. Most home stylists will go out on a limb and remove TVs from photos, but they're becoming increasingly harder to lift and take out of shot, and all that wiring means that by doing so we run the risk of accidentally knocking the family's lifeline Foxtel connector out.

You can't get rid of all that technology we can't seem to live without, but you can live with it by using either reveal or conceal tactics. The best reveal I've seen was a wall-mounted screen set among artworks. The set was a sensible size (that's to say there were artworks bigger than it), which meant that it was slightly cameo-ed within the larger context of the wall space. Another fabulous device I spotted was a TV target (ask your audio specialist) that uses infrared to cooperate with Foxtel, DVD, VCR and CD players so that people can watch something from one of these devices without their screen necessarily being in the same room. The target itself is inoffensive – double bonus! If you have to have a big set, a good way to counterbalance its size is with a visual decoy, such as an artwork or, as in this photo, a mirror that is slightly larger than the set.

If you'd rather take the conceal path and you're not bound by budget, pop-ups are the obvious choice. Drop-down projector screens are also an option. Built-in cabinetry provides the bulk of business for most furniture manufacturers, and television-lovers are spoilt for choice at both ends of the market. Regardless of your reveal or conceal tendencies, a Cable Turtle (available at rushfaster.com.au) is mandatory to keep your cords in a streamlined rather than an ad hoc mess.

Comparing televisions with such objects as Barinas will help you win the fight over what is a reasonable size for a television. Another way to keep it all in perspective is to compare the price of the desired set with an all-inclusive European holiday.

The art of simplification

Some people get away with decorative murder. Take nuns, for example: bless them and their immaculate dwellings. Or Shakers, another group who get off lightly when it comes to matters of the home. I don't know many nuns or Shakers, but there's no doubt they look content and happy in photos, so they must be doing something right! Simplifying your rooms is a laudable goal – it's just that not many people ever get there, let alone start trying.

Why *do* we clutter our living spaces with so much stuff? I'm not sure why other people do, but all I can say is that I just *love* stuff. Mad about it. Can't do without it, actually. But there's another theory, that filling our home with things can help to make us feel like a fully formed person. As a full-time buyer of stuff, I feel no shame in sharing this beautifully simple Aboriginal saying: The more you know, the less you need. Oh so true, but I'm still happy to go on knowing less if it means I might be able to have more. For others, however, this saying is a beacon of decorative hope.

This realm of interior decoration relies on quality not quantity. Provenance and pedigree help it work, since the few chosen pieces really do have to hold their own. If the job of art is to chase away ugliness, then rooms thoughtfully and artfully dressed surely make the home an artist. To pull simplicity off, you'll need to address only the most basic elements of the room in question – the seating, floor-covering and lighting. Everything else will subtract from its simplicity.

If simple is your thing, keep these four tips in mind:

1. It's best to follow a traditional placement of furniture: no wonky angles or kooky arrangements.
2. Furniture with deliberate lines and shapes work best. Their purity and form are most appreciated when they're not side by side with other furniture.
3. Use a neutral paint colour such as an eggshell or an extra-weak latte rather than white, so that the room doesn't look like a gallery.
4. A room without distractions can come across as boring, so use pattern or prints to liven it up, but bear in mind that these will always take centre stage. Patterned sofas can look amazing, but they do have a tendency to go a bit 'posh rental' on you.

Whatever your degree of success, comfort yourself with these facts: true style has no rules and simplicity is probably something we should all aim for.

Keeping it all spick and span

As this is an interiors book, not a housekeeping one, I'm reluctant to speak of such basic, non-decorating matters, but I feel that the topic of cleaning is vital enough for me to go out on a limb. There are many ways to skin this cat. Some people are born cleaners (Virgos or 'I can't sit here and relax while this place is such a mess' types). Some are learned cleaners (full-time boarders or 'My flatmate/husband/mother/partner has to have it just so' types). Some delegate the job but supervise the result (they have Absolute Domestics on speed dial).

No matter how the job gets done, there's enough research to prove that a tidy house can improve your state of being. At Montessori Schools they teach these fundamentals, because as far as Dr Maria Montessori was concerned, a tidy desk and work area are intrinsic to learning. If it's so damned important, then why is it so impossibly hard to do? We all know we should down 4 litres of water and exercise daily; its their very obviousness that makes these such undesirable tasks.

I'm a believer in sticking to where your strengths lie – if I did all the housework I'm supposed to, I'd never get to leave the house. So I take the bigger picture approach, always looking beyond the mess and dust – until someone threatens to come over. (Being self-employed also helps with this. I've trained myself to walk over the washing and ignore all ledges and surfaces until the onset of dust-induced sneezing attacks.) I know all too well that the road to cleaning perfection is a slippery slope. You start tending to just the basics, and before you know it you're following visitors with a back-Vac, taking their footprint treads out of the carpet.

Cleaning, like anything, works well when performed consistently. The following, given to me by a friend who's a professional housekeeper for an extremely wealthy family, is by no means a 'must do' list, but I've found it to be invaluable – life-changing no, but time-efficient yes:

- Weekly – Mop or vacuum floors, wipe counters, clean toilets, change sheets.
- Fortnightly – Dust furniture, clean shower.
- Monthly – Vacuum upholstery, dust moulding.
- Every three months – Turn over mattresses, wipe down ceiling-fan blades.
- Every four to six months – Clean fridge, polish appliances, scrub tile grout, wipe down cupboard fronts.

There is, of course, a yearly list and beyond (rug care, oven, windows, unwashable upholstery), but if I included that it would just make cleaning feel like a burden!

The best tip I've ever had came from the daughter of a homeowner whose house I photographed for a magazine. I asked the little girl how she kept her room so beautiful and clean. (Usually the answer is something like, 'My mother made me because you were coming.') 'I only do one thing at a time,' was her response. So true! So insightful! She might have been only six, but she already knew that prevention was the key to keeping on top of it all.

How to be insanely practical

A lot of people ask for help decorating their home, with a view to putting their house's best foot forward. What they often don't realise is that much of how their house feels has to do with the state of its organisation. When everything's full to the brim and not well set-up from the outset, chances are you'll think your house is letting you down or isn't right. In fact, even the worst house can perform better with some internal sorting.

I've identified seven stations (five if you don't have kids) you must create if you want to reach the dizzy heights of über-organisation. Freakily organised people will welcome this seven-step-to-heaven program and find it insanely practical. Others will be angered by its time-wasting anal-retentiveness.

Take them or leave them, but they might just improve the internal state of your home:

1. Destination station – This is where you put all your things down when you come in. I converted the coat cupboard in my entrance into a mini mud room – went crazy on hooks, hangers, boxes – and it feels oh-so-good.
2. Communication station – This is where you keep the messages, mail and other communications that make the house work. It's basically a glorified version of what you stick on your fridge, but arranged in greater detail so it's easier to find what you need without flipping through the pizza specials.
3. Admin station – This is the home office, where bills are kept and calls are made, medical rebates and consent forms filed and cheque book stowed. File your papers either alphabetically (by person, problem or supplier) or by month.
4. Gift station – It's the height of luxury to have one of these. Scissors, sticky tape, beautiful cards, ribbon, wrapping paper and back-up gifts are all kept here. In most cases, this station is a box, a drawer or even a cupboard, but in my wet dreams mine is a whole room.
5. Donation station – This is a general dumping-ground. A donation box that any member of the household can add to makes it easier when you finally get the impetus for a massive clean-out.
6. Education station – A box or a well-organised drawer, this should comprise all the tools necessary for undertaking homework, including good lighting, spare paper and some quiet if possible.
7. Creation station – This is usually only a small station, but it should contain everything kids need to create with (think the *Play School* Useful Box) – paints, art smocks, plenty of drawing instruments, scissors, paper, toilet rolls and glue.

Making do

'Don't move, improve' is sure to become the mantra for our times. It's a catchy little line and works a treat at band-aiding over any problem you might have with your own residence. Now that the days of house-flicking (continually turning lesser properties into Cinderellas for profit) are over, we're all basically stuck with what I call the 'givens'. The givens can be a range of things, but they'll most likely come in the form of:

- Things your spouse or flatmates won't let you throw out, givens you have to work around.
- Items that are temporarily out of your price range: 'It's a given that we have to live with this lounge until we can afford the imported one.'
- Pieces that you have to keep for sentimental or ethical reasons because they were bequeathed to you.

Once you've accepted the givens (no matter what they are), home life can suddenly become a little easier – and you're free to get rid of all your other junk. At the time it might feel like a roll-over tactic, but I see it more as a coping mechanism. Nothing is forever. And you can always reupholster, repaint, rechrome, recane, revamp or reformat. The givens in my house are usually bound by budget. I'll work with the lounge until I find my dream sofa because I'm in love with my chocolaty floors. And if all goes well and my budget is accurate, I'll be sitting pretty on my new lounge very soon.

Another given you might have to live with is your house's unfortunate orientation. It might be a given that you have to put up with a dark, damp space, so what should you do? Work with opposites to make it as light and airy as possible – mirrors and white paint with reflective properties will do the trick.

Another given could be walls that need to be moved or rooms you'd like to open up but you can't afford it right at this moment. These are the hardest of all givens, requiring the most patience. You must work with them and know that there *is* light at the end of the tunnel.

One key coping mechanism is the power of conceding. By this I mean conceding that the furniture you've invested in for now might not be what you want once you've actually removed the wall, extended the roof line and installed your gorgeous new bi-folds. And then the givens just keep on coming. What was once a reaction to a given, becomes one itself.

Acceptance, you see, is the key!

Living with pets

Pets will change the way your house works, but always for the better. Events planner and animal-lover Jamie Gordon says if you get a cat you should prepare to be ignored, but if you get a dog your life will never be the same. You can forget long sleep-ins – 'unless you have a British bulldog,' says Jamie (they are apparently 'charmingly lazy').

The best thing about living with animals? They don't notice whether you're old, ill or unsuccessful – to them you're just perfect. Apparently, one of the measures of our downwards-sliding society is our inability to care for the world at large. Instead, they say, we are turning inwards and spoiling our pets. I have a theory, though, that if you're generally nice to animals, you're more likely to be nice to other people. Dogs are incapable of hiding their true feelings, but sometimes, as in my best friend's case, having a cat is a bit like having a bad boyfriend. She comes home after a hard day's work to a reluctant greeting from her cat, Ruby, who scratches and claws her in an attempt to engage in some soft play and then expects full meals and board. It's just the kind of cat Ruby is.

Cats *are* largely a law unto themselves, but here are some pointers for new cat parents:

- If cat scratching is a problem, look at what your cat enjoys scratching and see if you can find a substitute. If he loves pulling apart your best pillows, then get him an old pillow of his very own, one that you won't mind him destroying.
- Cats like chewing all manner of things. Try giving her some toys with leather laces, so she has something you don't mind her chewing.
- While your cuddly kitten might be all smoochy and purring at home, most cats are serious predators, hunting many native animals. Buy a collar with a bell to give the wildlife a chance, and try and keep your cats inside, especially at night.

Whether you're a cat or dog person (who could resist this pooch, though?), the kind of person who gives their pets the same residential rights as humans or you subscribe to the 'them outside/us inside' school of thought, the marketplace is positively swamped with ploys to tempt you to spend. But if the thought of spending huge sums on a pooch, moggy or any other pet upsets you, you can support a needy family by buying a pig for $50 or a sheep for $157 from caregifts.org.au.

If you have a pet in an apartment, the petloo.com.au is an ingenious invention – albeit an eyesore (let's face it, most pet products, no matter how practical, usually are) – that works a treat.

For more on pampering your pooch, turn over for 'Living with a dog – really!'.

Living with a dog – really!

When I first wrote a column about living with pets, I was forced to apologise to every single pet-owning reader who had to suffer my ill-informed, ignorant remarks on the subject. Now I have a puppy all of my own, I must right my wrongs. Here are some lessons I've learnt:

- Whatever you have in your house, you must be prepared to sacrifice it. Teething pups don't know the difference between your $500 ballet shoes and the $20 cheapos you bought when passing Erina Fair on the way home from holidays. They don't know mahogany from birch, either. In fact, they don't even know a furniture leg from an architrave. Yesterday my dog actually ate the kitchen wall – that's how desperate they are to numb their gums. A sprinkle of lavender oil supposedly works to deter some dogs from furniture, rugs and no-go areas, but it's useless with mine. At less than $5 a bottle, however, it's a fairly risk-free option.
- I am a big fan of Ikea, but they should really not be allowed to sell those $7.95 Bästis dog baskets without admitting that they are a red flag as far as a teething pup goes. It took mine three and a half weeks to eat it down to nothing. Buy four pig's ears from your friendly butcher instead. Your pooch will chew them, sharpen his teeth on them, bury them, dig them up and start all over again – that's a whole lot of fun for $2 each.
- You'll find your own dog-parenting feet, but err on the side of Victorian discipline. It's a hard line, but the stricter you are now the sweeter it'll be later.
- Living with a puppy is like living with a toddler – you have to keep the floor picked up. A puppy will soon find that staple, pin, rubber band or paperclip.
- Get the videos by Cesar Millan (Oprah's dog-trainer). I'm sure there are more suitable and sensible Australian dog-training DVDs, but Caesar's American clientele and their neurotic dogs will make you feel so much better about your own.
- Mid-brown floors are your best defence against unsightly dog hairs if you really care about them that much. Otherwise, get to know the Ergorapido from Electrolux (electrolux.com.au).
- Don't set up a prearranged dog area: it will only lead to disappointment. I made mine picture-perfect but he just walked straight past and found his own corner.

If you don't want to spend absurd amounts of money on a pet of your own and you've already donated at caregifts.org.au, you could give generously to the RSPCA (rspca.org.au) to help pets less fortunate than those I've been talking about.

Here are some dog-friendly things a new dog parent could try:

- Lamb, Mushy Pea & Mint Cookies from Jollie (jollie.com.au).
- Magis Dog House from Top 3 by Design (top3.com.au).
- Fat Boy Bed from Moggy and Mutt (moggyandmutt.com.au).
- IRuvYou pewter pet tag from Bowhouse (bowhouse.com.au).
- Bästis food bowl from Ikea (ikea.com.au).

Presentation is all when selling

As anyone who's ever sold their home can tell you, the house always looks its best the day it gets its photos taken. How is it that a poorly orientated, drab two-and-a-bit bedder suddenly becomes *the* most incredible residence? Whether we take them for granted or not, we supposedly hang onto material things because we see them as a measure of our worth, so passing on a house to someone else can be very difficult. Then, just at the moment you know it's never going to be yours again, there it is, staring you in the face with its best dress on.

There's a whole army of stylists out there who work exclusively in the real-estate sector. Called 'stagers', these magicians turn hovels like mine into homes. Armed with space-saving devices, secret techniques and potions, they make even the air more saleable. They also know all about eye-trickery – ways to deploy the glance from a dated fitting to a covetable object. And they do all this within a short timeframe to a set budget.

Never one to withhold information, here are my top six discoveries from my research into real-estate styling:

1. We usually push the furniture back to the walls to make the room appear bigger, but the professionals suggest pulling furniture *away* from the walls, so that prospective buyers can see the corners of the rooms.
2. Always clean the windows. It's the sort of thing that people don't notice – the house will just 'feel' clean.
3. People love to open a cupboard here, test a door there. With this in mind, ensure your robes are half-full and that the bottom of the closet is visible. Show people a jam-packed wardrobe and they'll think it's too small for them, too.
4. Spend money where it matters, out the front. That's where the property makes its first impression and where most of the negotiations will take place.
5. Go easy on the flowers. Put them only where you'd expect to see them. Yes, only real ones are allowed. And no, a bowl of fruit does not replace flowers. For a long-lasting display, ask your florist for ginger sticks, chincherinchees, lotus pods, king proteas, flowering gum, callicarpa or Gymea lilies. Magnolia, hellebore and olive foliage are all perfect for long-lasting foliage-only displays.
6. Lose what stagers term 'visual dandruff' – newspapers, mail and laundry. Basically, in the real-estate market, clutter eats up equity.

No one knows your house better than you do, though. Charm and warmth, a valuable commodity, will get under the viewers' skin and be something they're willing to pay for.

Resale research tells us that an upstairs attic area makes your house more covetable. It also says that houses with flagpoles command a higher price! I love that a flagpole would be a positive attribute to a home's sales potential – how kooky but encouraging all the same. I don't know many houses (outside the USA) with flagpoles, but I do love flags. See flagsfantastic.com.au for some to make a cushion from, frame and hang on a wall or stick on a flagpole at the front of your house to impress buyers!

How to entertain

Some people really know how to live, and it's these people who are usually very adept entertainers – gracious and generous hosts. Once you take a closer look at their modus operandi, you'll find that much of it rests in their ability to lay on an effortless spread, no matter how short-order or deliberately decadent it might be. If, for you, sharing food with friends is one of life's simple pleasures, surely summer is the ideal season in which to do it, regardless of your culinary skill set.

For those of you (okay, for those of us) for whom entertaining is not a god-given talent (my feeling is it's like being naturally good at French or driving), this is where the good fortune of timing kicks in. Summer, being the all-round-good-time sexy season it is, provides the ideal opportunity to entertain risk-free. It's time to go out on an entertaining limb while the butterflies are fluttering, the frangipanis are in flower, your white sheets are being sun-dried and even south-west facing houses seem light-filled. One dish is a little overcooked? Aaahh, not to worry, just soak up that glorious sunshine and pour another drink.

When you *do* venture to a table outside, the most important things to get right (apart from the food and company, of course) are the implements and elements. Shade is compulsory – a market umbrella can not only add a splash of colour but save your guests from nearly fainting. When it comes to the actual table top, most people assume that outdoor options stop at picnic-related pieces. Not so. This season the market is flush with unbreakable, dishwashable pieces that mimic the style and form of their indoor counterparts. Naff? Not a chance. Plastic is the new ceramic and comes in many glamorous guises, turning its back on its humble suburban history. For every piece you use inside, there's a plastic (or melamine) version for outdoors in great shapes and colours you'd never be game to try inside. Sprinkle magic over any old table top with tropical colours. (A word to the wise: don't over-use orange or your table will look like a tribute to Tang.)

That said, I'm a firm believer that all food looks (and tastes) better when eaten off white plates – so I use the coloured pieces as under-plates, side plates and serving dishes. If you want a little more bone in your china, intermix the plastics with your Wedgwood. Jasper Conran's Casual range (jasperconran.com) is a great option here – it's microwave-, freezer- and dishwasher-proof, yet has the looks of a pedigreed restaurant plate. Let loose! Summer entertaining is all in the mix.

For more on the perfect do, see 'The ultimate garden party' on page 196 and 'A cheat sheet for partying' on page 198.

Okay to party on? Do a weather check at bom.gov.au – stylists, party-planners and photographers all swear by it. For the best (and cheapest) outdoor seating, try the Evert stool in yellow, green or black from Ikea (ikea.com.au) – stackable, and weather-resistant, it's perfect for outdoor gatherings.

The ultimate garden party

My guru on matters domestic, Melissa Penfold, has a great tip for entertaining effortlessly: an elegant hostess is a calm hostess. By all means kill yourself delivering three courses of fine dining to a dozen friends, but you could book a table at your favourite restaurant and actually have fun instead. If you're lucky enough to have your own garden, though, there's no excuse for not entertaining outside when spring comes around. An impromptu party in the garden, under a tree, lets you off the hook with food (I've noticed that people generally lower their expectations when they eat outside), but also relieves you decoratively. Preparation time is minimal and, as long as the sun keeps shining, you really run no risk of failure.

The only possible threat is overdoing it. It's easy to tip over from casual elegance into ridiculous if you're not careful. Here are a few tried-and-tested tips:

- Never put bouquets of flowers outside. Teeny-tiny posies in small, low-to-the-table vessels are okay.
- Don't water the lawn on the morning of the party: chairs and shoes can sink in if the ground is too moist.
- If it will take more than half an hour to make it, prepare it or arrange it, forget it – garden parties are meant to be about less stress/high impress.
- Iced tea is party-perfect. Try T2's herbal tisanes served on ice with a sprig of mint.
- Be brave. It's all about getting away with the things you could never do inside.
- Put a bin behind a tree so you can deal with all the rubbish straightaway.
- Consider setting up a breakaway rug on the ground for snoozes, conversations and fun. Or set up a tent for the children using an old sheet and three garden stakes tied together at the top with rope or twine, tepee-style.
- Use a tree for shade and for hanging up bunting, decorations or lanterns.
- Personalise the place-settings with messages, names or thoughts from nametapes.com.au.
- Always buy two more bottles of wine or bubbly than you think you'll need.
- Have lap blankets, pashminas and wraps on hand in case it turns cold.
- Could you ever say no to an ice-cream sandwich? It's the perfect ending to a garden party. (My feeling is only vanilla will do – stick with the classics.)
- If something *does* fail you, keep on smiling no matter what.

For more tips on entertaining with panache, see 'How to entertain' on page 194 and 'A cheat sheet for partying' on page 198.

Here are some more fail-safe, no-recipe sweet endings:

- Figs steeped in rosewater.
- Store-bought granita piled into wide glasses.
- Store-bought macaroons with a trio of summer teas.
- A watermelon injected with vodka and frozen.

A cheat sheet for partying

Okay, this is the lazy person's guide to garnering entertaining accolades. I've worked on lunches that cost thousands of dollars a head as well as sniff-of-an-oily-rag occasions, but they both share the same ingredients for success:

1. Only serve seasonally. If it's not tomato season, don't be doing bruschetta.
2. Do one thing but in huge volumes. I love buying a hundred oysters and piling them around tiered cake stands with lemon wedges – all in the middle of the table. Voilà – a decadent-looking edible centrepiece.
3. Delegate as much as you can without losing control. There's no prize for doing it all. No one wants to party with a stressed-out pressure pot.
4. Most people buy way too much ice. Put one bag back. Always. On the other hand, always put two extra bottles of bubbly/white/red/spirits on the trolley – you can never have enough.
5. Accept that food only ever looks good on white plates.
6. Have a wet-weather back-up plan. You should be able to strip down your arrangements easily and bump them indoors with minimum fuss.
7. If you have more than twelve dinner guests, consider getting help. The best money you can spend on a dinner is for a bartender. Black tee and pants only – a penguin suit will make them and you look like a right prat.
8. Stock up on toilet paper. It's amazing how much a dozen or so people can get through. Disturbing to think about, but ever so practical.
9. Consider a feature drink. If, like me, you're a less-than-skilled cook, this is vital.
10. If dinner feels like too much pressure, brunches and breakfasts are far less daunting, just as much fun and have a significantly lower alcohol bill.
11. If you live near a great cake shop or cafe, ask them to make you a larger sized version of their house specialty.
12. If you have, say, three gimmicks going on (such as feature lighting, a clever table top and nifty name tags) try to lose one. Better still, use just one idea but execute it beautifully and simply.
13. Know your strengths and put your best foot forward. My parties always have a subtle colour or theme so as to divert attention away from the food.

For more tips on finding your inner entertainer, see 'How to entertain' on page 194 and 'The ultimate garden party' on page 196.

The dishes with which I have most success all have zero cooking time. Try these three no-cook winners, perfect for people with no time, zero skill or, like me, a dangerous combination of both!

1. Peking duck – I get my local Chinese restaurant to cook and debone the duck, then sell me the pancakes, shallot sticks and jam. I serve it all with Asian beers – perfect.
2. Freshly shucked oysters with a chilly pinot.
3. Cherries with vanilla-bean ice-cream and espresso.

It's easy being green

Turning leftover garden into vegetable patch is admirable, and giving away any surplus produce is gallant. (See myfarmsf.com – a San Francisco business that takes people's backyard plots, farms them for those who don't have time and sells the surplus produce to the wider community.)

Here are some general actions you can take when decorating that could save the planet:

1. Walls – The paint industry is one of the world's most polluting. Water-based gloss requires dilutions of 1 million litres to 1 to render its entry into the sewerage system harmless. Try a paint made from plant oils instead.

2. Online purchases – As an online shopper, it's a small but significant step to opt for surface mail rather than a speedy delivery service. Shopping is the ultimate power, and our small purchases add up into new buying patterns that manufacturers will notice.

3. New builds – Don't go for halogen downlighting if you can help it. It might be labelled low-voltage, but it uses more energy than a standard 60-watt light globe. If you're stuck with halogen downlights, change them to fluorescent downlights using a $19.95 kit from neco.com.au.

4. Office – Tudor Eco DL envelopes are Australian-made (so have fewer carbon miles) from 100 per cent post-consumer recycled board and paper, and sold in a box made from 100 per cent post-consumer recycled fibre. Try printing in ecofont, a Dutch-designed sans-serif typeface that wastes no ink on serif flourishes – download it free from ecofont.eu.

5. Heating – Insulating your roof can save you thousands on heating bills. In fact, you're likely not to need to turn your heating on at all. And wouldn't you much rather spend your money on a delicious Hermès orange Avalon H blanket than heating?

The sooner we all implement our own measures the better, because if we continue ploughing through our ecosystems the way we have been, there's a really good chance there'll be no butterflies (not to mention the plant life that depends on them) by the year 2100. And that's really, really sad.

Weekender heaven

I had a weekender once. It gave me some of the best weekends of my life, allowing me to neglect completely my permanent place of residence and to live in permanent denial by beautifying a space we lived in for sometimes as little as twelve hours a week.

What I love about having a second residence/weekender/place in the country/house at the beach is that you can very easily get away with pure fantasy decorating. The lounge only has to hold up for two days, so you can have it upholstered in a loud vintage peony print, one that you could clearly never tolerate Monday to Friday after a hard day's work. Your inevitably mismatched plates and crockery will look random and charming in a second house. The bedcovers can be crazy, multicoloured and all the same, something your family members would be up in arms about at your real home. And you can fill the garden with things you'd never have the nerve to disturb your neighbourhood with at your real home.

But best of all is that you suddenly get extra rooms, walls, shelves and nooks for all that *stuff*. This is great news if you like to buy lots of things but you can't necessarily get away with displaying them at home. I've seen many a weekender – whose owners live quite classically at their real home – playing host to a ginormous shell collection or ridiculous amounts furniture made from twigs.

When I had my weekender, I found myself sniffing around for red kitchen enamel. That proved way too easy to find, so I narrowed it down to kitchen enamel in red-and-white polka dots. The race was on, and it wasn't long before the display cabinet was full to the point of stupid. Then I started on antique jelly moulds. Hung on the otherwise bare wall, their chiselled bottoms became works of art, making beautiful and honest silhouettes. I realised it was time to stop when I had enough to cover the walls of three whole rooms. That's what you get when you rise to the challenge of decorating the house with items that cost no more than double digits. A $99 limit makes you think harder, but it also frees you up to make mistakes and follow silly decorative whims.

The best thing about weekenders? All that ever lingers in your memory during the week are your blooming flower beds, your incredibly nifty decorating and those relaxing soaks in your claw-footed tub. Somehow the more practical aspects of owning a weekender – like the pilgrimages to hardware stores, having to buy two of everything or forking out for two separate electricity bills – recede and make way for all the nice stuff. Make the most of the fun side by buying up big on super-soft cushions, whimsical window dressings and lots of blankets.

For weekend-only buys try:

- A natural bamboo door curtain (90 × 200 centimetres) from My Island Home (myislandhome.com.au).
- Shweshwe cushions from Shweshwe (shweshwe.com).
- And, of course, board games such as Hungry Hungry Hippos, Jenga, Boggle or Monopoly Here and Now: The Australian Edition. Games were made for the weekend!

but wait,
there's more

how high should you go? Some ergonomic rules

There are some things you just need to know and one of them is what's deemed to be 'standard', especially if you want something that isn't. For instance, did you know that doorknobs are usually set 92 centimetres high? Now this is good information if you want to make yours super-high (for deliberate elegance) or super-low.

In the same vein of helpful but hard-to-come-by information, here are some more numbers to know:

- The standard height for a desk is 74 centimetres, for a counter 92 centimetres (although this is becoming increasingly higher), and for a bar 1.07 metres. Ideally, the height of the chair or stool to go with these should correspond and be at least 25–30 centimetres lower.
- Most coffee tables are 46 centimetres high, and you should leave an 8 centimetre gap between the sofa and your end tables.
- A standard chair is 46 centimetres high, so for the comfort of those sitting at the table the underside of your dining table should not be lower than 66 centimetres.
- Bookcases should be 30–38 centimetres deep and a working desk (not just a pretty one) at least 60 centimetres deep.
- Your headboard (if you have an upholstered bed head) should be at least 60–68 centimetres higher than the top of your mattress.
- The optimal television-viewing distance depends of course on the size of your set, but as a general rule (based on guidelines developed by the Society of Motion Pictures and Television Engineers), the distance between you and your big screen should be no less than about twice the screen width and no more than five times the screen width. For a 76 centimetre screen, then, the minimum viewing distance is about 2.3 metres, while for a 165 centimetre screen it's about 5 metres. This rule of thumb doesn't necessarily represent the ideal home-theatre viewing distance, but indicates the optimal limits.
- Most doors are 2.1 metres high. This is based on the proportions of the human body and an opening through which an average person feels comfortable passing. If I'm working with a new building, I love raising doors above the standard height (never lowering them) – it fools the eye into thinking the ceiling is higher than it is.

every flower in its season

Home-making and flowers go hand in hand. I work with my friend Lisa Cooper whose service, The Butcher's Daughter, makes the most beautiful arrangements using whatever is seasonally available. Here's a list she gave me. Find your favourite flower, diarise it and get onto your florist!

JANUARY – figs on branches, gardenia, nepenthes (pitcher plants)
For me, gardenias are as beautiful when they're first cut as they are on their way out. I always keep them as they brown – their scent just seems to develop and deepen.

FEBRUARY – basil, hydrangea, love-lies-bleeding, waterlily
I put love-lies-bleeding in a cut-crystal vase up high and let it cascade down the side of my cupboard.

MARCH – autumn hydrangea, mint, parrot tulips
Mint should be everywhere – admired, eaten, drunk and drifting on the breeze through an open window.

APRIL – pomegranate, rosehip, violet leaves
I'm like a queen with grape hyacinth, holding onto it in a nosegay or a tussie mussie. Its scent is sublime.

MAY – autumn leaves, peppercorn, poppy
Autumn leaves are unequivocally emotive and their scale is commanding.

JUNE – anemone, Canterbury bell, holly, violet
A mass of anemones in a glass vase with a cut slipper orchid as an accent is very narrative. Think Lewis Carroll.

JULY – daphne, hellebore, smokebush, sweet pea
Hellebore is like a rambling rose. Have it en masse – as much as you can carry in two arms is good!

AUGUST – apple blossom, slipper orchid, sweet William
Slipper orchids potted in a baking tray and covered in moss are like cranky little men in an argument – it's really something!

SEPTEMBER – bluebell, grape hyacinth, ranunculus
Ranunculus sits very well in eclectic vessels – put water in anything you can find and drop little masses of them in each.

OCTOBER – dogwood, guelder rose, lilac, lily-of-the-valley
Try lily-of-the-valley in a little water glass. It won't last long, but while it does it will be extraordinary.

NOVEMBER – bearded iris, 'Julia's rose', peony
Peonies are considered the *king* of the flower kingdom. They're majestic. Just keep changing their water and giving them a little trim.

DECEMBER – crabapple, fir tree, Queen Anne's lace
You may need to drive for a while to find a beautiful Christmas tree. Do.

ALL YEAR – African violets in pots, baby's breath, carnation, garden roses, tortured willow. Carnations and baby's breath need to be kept separate. Both will have their day, again, and I think that day may be upon us.

the world's best bookshops

I got into styling and all matters of the home by way of books, and they are both my greatest indulgence and an absolute necessity. One of my life goals is to get to every one of these bookshops. If you love books too, drop me a line with your favourite bookshop (megan@meganmorton.com) – I'd love to add it to my to-do list!

1. **Shakespeare and Company** (37 rue de la Bûcherie, 75005 Paris, France; shakespeareandcompany.com) – It doesn't get better than this. There are thirteen beds in this shop and 40 000 people have slept here. You won't believe it until you've seen it.

2. **Atlantis Books** (Oia Santorini, TK 84702, Cyclades, Greece; atlantisbooks.org) – Run by a collective of artists, writers and activists, Atlantis is as beautiful as the surrounding deep blue seas.

3. **Bookartbookshop** (17 Pitfield St, London N1 6HB, UK; bookartbookshop.com) – It's here you realise the power and potential of books.

4. **Selexyz Dominicanen** (Dominikanerkerkstraat 1, Universiteitssingel 30, Maastricht, The Netherlands; selexyz.nl/winkels/38/maastricht/domikanerstraat-1) – What does a Dutch city do with an 800-year-old church that has no congregation? Convert it into a temple of books, of course.

5. **El Ateneo Grand Splendid** (Avenida Santa Fé 1860, Buenos Aires, Argentina; tematika. com/sucursales) – An old theatre turned into bookshop, where the theatre boxes have been converted into teeny reading rooms. Incredible!

6. **Strand Books** (828 Broadway [at 12th St], New York, USA; strandbooks.com) – It's one of the big guys but there's nothing better than beating jetlag in the Strand aisles.

7. **Posada Art Books** (rue de la Madeleine 29, 1000 Brussels, Belgium; posada.be) – Interiors to die for and impressive second-hand art books on offer.

8. **Cafebrería El Péndulo in Mexico** (pendulo.com) – The Polanco branch (Alejandro Dumas 81, Colonia Polanco, Mexico City, Mexico) has an open-air area populated with several trees, to which you can escape to pore over the books.

9. **Keibunsha** (10 Ichijyoji haraitono-cho, Sakyo-ku, Kyoto 606-8184, Japan; keibunshabooks.com) – The quiet dignity of Keibunsha is what makes it so ludicrously beautiful.

10. **Hatchards Bookshop** (187 Piccadilly, London W1J 9LE, UK; hatchards.co.uk) – Six floors of heaven, trading since 1797. Go there knowing that the likes of Byron and Wilde were once regulars.

resources

I'm a lucky duck because I've been able to source the world for beautiful things through my decorating business, HOME, as well as through shopping for my styling work. No matter how well planned my trips are, I always find that there is never enough time. There are already too many expansive guidebooks and fashiony–luxe travel guides out there detailing every shop, so I thought a nice way to end HOME LOVE would be to take a quick whizz around the world's best design destinations.

I've kept this list strictly to retail outlets, imagining that you have only one full day up your sleeve. For some cities I've included pit stops, others just great lobbies or public spaces you need to see (as you can glean lots of ideas for your home from fabulous hotels and restaurants, remember!).

The South of France (Fayence in particular) is a favourite of mine, and I am happy to email you my top picks of the local stores if you're ever travelling that way (email me at megan@meganmorton. com). My in-laws live there and my mother-in-law has knockout taste, so half of my favourites are her local haunts. I figure, though, that you're more likely to find yourself in Sydney, Melbourne, London, Paris, Milan, New York or Tokyo, so please enjoy these great spots.

Sydney

If I dropped in from Mars and was allowed half a day before the space-ship took off again, here's where I would go to experience Sydney's decorative style.

The Country Trader
PYD Building, 197 Young St, Waterloo NSW 2017; (02) 9698 4661; thecountrytrader.com.au
A direct portal to Europe, merchandised oh-so Sydney-style. While you're there, have a Ruben sandwich or a reliable coffee at Dank Street Depot (danksstreetdepot.com. au), which is in the same complex, and then whizz around the area's various galleries, which offer both Indigenous and white Australian art. To see what's on gallery-wise, visit 2danksstreet. com.au.

Koskela
Level 1, Imperial Slacks Building, 91 Campbell St, Surry Hills NSW 2010; (02) 9280 0999; koskela.com.au
Koskela is unique in supporting Australian and New Zealand ecological and sustainable design in furniture, bedding, objects and gifts without being overly earnest. In fact, you'd never know it was environmentally minded – it presents as one of Sydney's most exciting retail stores. Defying the laws of retail, it's not on the ground floor, but then again, most of Koskela's initiatives and products aren't run-of-the-mill. In my eyes, Koskela sums up Sydney perfectly.

Parterre Garden
33 Ocean St, Woollahra NSW 2025; (02) 9363 5874; parterre.com.au
This place never disappoints. Ever. Housed in one of Woollahra's important, double-fronted sandstone corner shops, it also has two stories, so a visit guarantees a relaxing stroll from room to room, floor to floor. It also has a suitably beautiful outdoor area. The displays go beyond the realm of 'visual merchandising', taking it to a whole new level.

davidmetnicole
382 Cleveland St, Surry Hills NSW 2010; (02) 9698 7416; davidmetnicole.com
For small items of real interest that are one part Portobello, two parts Sydney. And while you're in the area, wander down the road to number 267 for John Williams's madcap Mao and More (maoandmore.com), an Asian mecca brimming with wit, good humour and oriental pieces.

Icebergs Dining Room and Bar
1 Notts Ave, Bondi Beach NSW 2026; (02) 9365 9000; idrb.com
Finish your day in Sydney with a G&T, sitting in the hanging wicker Nanna Ditzel egg chair at Icebergs and taking in the ultimate drinking view. It's so superbly Sydney but also a great place to witness the interior beauty of sea-foam green and blue (the colour of Icebergs' soft furnishings).

Melbourne

To understand Melbourne is to shop for the home there. Melbourne works in less obvious ways than Sydney, so expect surprises and laneway discoveries. I think of Melbourne as very discreet and very well served, with lots of choice.

Geoffrey Hatty Applied Arts
296 Malvern Rd, Prahran Vic. 3181; (03) 9510 1277
This place best sums up Melbourne's chic vision for dressing the home for me. I adore this exquisite double store. It makes me want to move to an art deco apartment and start all over again. Filled with twentieth-century furniture but without the usual suspects, it's just a pleasure to be in.

Angelucci 20th Century
92 High St, Windsor Vic. 3181; (03) 9525 1271; angelucci.net.au.
Angelucci really does scour the globe to bring back the chicest of mid-century offerings. A little bit of all nations is represented – not just Danish, French or Italian. The only prerequisite is that the item be beautiful.

Izzi and Popo
258 Ferrars St, South Melbourne Vic. 3205; (03) 9696 1771; izziandpopo.com.au
This place has beautiful treasures from Europe and beyond, all displayed against gold-striped walls. Find everything from tea sets and framed butterflies to larger furniture, all with patina and charm.

Tarlo and Graham
60 Chapel St, Windsor Vic. 3181; (03) 9521 2221; tarloandgraham.com
Character pieces with a semi-industrial spin are to be found here. It sums up Melbourne's tolerance for eclectic interior pieces.

Empire Vintage
63 Cardigan Pl., Albert Park Vic. 3206; (03) 9682 6677; empirevintage.com.au
This store front for Melbourne identity Lyn Gardener has furniture and vintage-inspired knick-knacks downstairs, and clothes and accessories upstairs. Lyn has an endless supply

of goodies (think milk glass, old signage, commodes, chairs, glassware, chandeliers, bunting), so it's unlikely you'll see the same object there twice. If vintage is your thing, Lyn also hosts a fabulous specialised shopping tour (avintageouting.com) from a sweet Fiat 500.

Pearl Café
599 Church St, Richmond Vic. 3121; (03) 9427 1307

If you find yourself hungry while checking out my recommendations, then just across the river and, surrounded by other great home outlets (RG Madden, Space and Poliform showrooms), you'll find the Pearl Café.

New Gold Mountain
21 Liverpool St, Melbourne Vic. 3000; (03) 9650 8859; newgoldmountain.org

For suitably fancy cocktails at the end of a hard day's shopping, go down a cobbled laneway, through a red door and down some rickety stairs, and you will find (fingers crossed!) New Gold Mountain channelling 1920s Shanghai glamour. Drink it in, it's wonderful!

London

With an English husband and lots of fun cousins and friends to visit in the Old Dart, I often find myself pining for London's superior retail environs. To me, the English have retail down to perfection, despite their sometimes stuffy service.

Few and Far
242 Brompton Rd, London SW3 2BB; +44 20 7225 7070; fewandfar.net

My favourite London store is from tastemaker Priscilla Carluccio. It's hard to pigeonhole Few and Far – every time I go there it's so different. Needless to say, I promise you'll find things here that you'd never see anywhere else in the world. So very

in touch with what homes need, it even has a flower shop at the side and beautiful coffee or tea for customers meandering around its two floors. You won't be disappointed. It's just beautiful.

Zara Home
129–131 Regent St, London W1B 4HT; +44 20 7432 0400; zarahome.com

Because I like to mix the top end with the bottom, I always like to pop in here. I believe that London does the top-end–low-end thing best, and Zara has the decorative edge at the bottom end. Find reasonably priced (even in pounds) linen, tabletop items and homewares that reflect the fashion featured at the front of the store.

The Conran Shop Chelsea
Michelin House, 81 Fulham Rd, London SW3 6RD; +44 20 7589 7401; conran.com

It's an English stalwart, but what I love most about a London trip is a truffle sandwich and a glass of something at Bibendum outside the garden-section entrance to the Conran Shop. I adore the bathroom, books, kids, cookware, outdoor and furniture sections, and even the card section is always inspiring.

The Cloth Shop
290 Portobello Rd, London W10 5TE; +44 20 8968 6001; theclothshop.net

Now in its fifteenth year, Portobello Road's only fabric shop sells an extensive range of natural furnishing fabrics, beautiful Swedish linens, antique European household goods and a wide selection of old and new woollen blankets. The best buy is Swedish furnishing linen (you're spoilt for choice with 24 colours) at just £15 per metre.

Labour and Wait
18 Cheshire St, London E2 6EH; +44 20 7729 6253; labourandwait.co.uk

You can view Labour and Wait's merchandise at Dover Street Market (doverstreetmarket.com), but I find DSM amazingly over-curated. Instead, I prefer to inspect Labour and Wait's

utilitarian take on household items in the charming confines of their own store. Simon Watkins and Rachel Wythe-Moran, the owners, continue to supply timeless, stylish and durable goods for the home.

Traditional Toy
Chelsea Green, 53 Godfrey St, London SW3 3SX; +44 20 7352 1718; traditionaltoy.com

I love the idea of old-school toys, although we all know that kids are likely to play with plastic ones with just as much vigour. I always like to visit Traditional Toy to pick up small handcrafted presents for my little ones back home.

Paul Smith (Furniture)
9 Albemarle St, London W1S 4BL; +44 20 7493 4564; paulsmith.co.uk

While better known for his fashion, Paul Smith has opened a new store in pretty Mayfair, selling art, antiques, jewellery and curiosities sourced from around the world. To label it as 'Paul Smith's home store' is to undermine its rarities, though. Trip over investment 1960s Murano glass chandeliers at £1850 or vintage screen-printed friezes from £359.

Flat White
17 Berwick St, London W1F 0PT; +44 20 7734 0370; flat-white.co.uk

Now while London might be the retail mecca, it falls short on coffee. Set up by Australians, Flat White is a must if you need a caffeine hit before you hit the shops.

Paris

Merci
111 blvd Beaumarchais, 75003 Paris; +33 1 4277 0033; merci-merci.com

There is a new ruler in retail and Merci is its name. My fingers can't type fast enough and my brain can't find enough superlatives to describe

how I feel about this store. I *will* tell you what was in my shopping basket last time I was there, just to show you Merci's scope: my own Annick Goutal fragrance (hand-bottled by me), new clothes for my unborn baby, a vintage scarf for me, a great roll of disposable (and washable) napkins, metres of lovely grey silk electrical flex so I can rewire my bathroom lights without resorting to the ugly plastic leads we have here, lots of delightful ribbon from the haberdashery section, and a beautiful hardback for €5 from the secondhand bookstore. All this, followed by a serve of boiled eggs and toast soldiers from an angelic waitress called Celeste. Le swoon! I even noted the specs for the best lounge I have ever seen.

Colette
213 rue Saint-Honoré, 75001 Paris; +33 1 5535 3390; colette.fr

I don't love the trainer-spruiking Colette, but it's kind of ungrateful not to go in for a little look-see. What I *do* like about Colette is that it's a walkable distance from beautiful boutiques such as Lanvin (lanvin. com) and Hermès (hermès.com), which has the most incredible visual merchandising in the universe.

7L
7 rue de Lille, 75007 Paris; +33 1 4292 0358

Paris has lots of beautiful bookshops, and a meander around town will lead you to your own favourites. I stumbled across a very chic and discreet one called 7L, not realising that it is Monsieur Karl Lagerfeld's very own store until I saw the fingerless-gloved, bejeweled Karl himself. 'I'm mad for books,' Karl has said. 'It is a disease I won't recover from. They are the tragedy of my life. I want to learn about everything.' I love this next bit: 'I want to know everything, but I'm not an intellectual, and I don't like their company. I'm the most superficial man on earth.' With nothing but fashion, design, art and garden titles, it's a great way to see the world's best design-related books all in the one compact store.

Les Puces de Paris Saint-Ouen

140 rue des Rosiers,
93400 Saint-Ouen;
+33 1 4012 3258;
parispuces.com

Spend half a day meandering through the Clignancourt flea market. Small purchases, major pieces, it all happens here. Paris has lots of markets, of course, but this one is so good both for first-timers and old hands. A seemingly bottomless pit of wonderful!

La Société

4 Place Saint-Germain-des-Prés,
75006 Paris; +33 1 5363 6060

This restaurant is serious and its design is the work of Christian Liaigre, one of the best in the world. It's sublime, just sublime.

Milan

Armani Casa Milano

Via Manzoni 37, 20121 Milan;
+39 02 657 2401; armanicasa.com

This is the fascist-style headquarters for everything zen, muted and clean-lined. Don't be put off by its severity – I just imagine loads of floppy parrot tulips, piles of books and pots of tea all strewn around! Once I've taken a breath downstairs and ooohed and ahhed at all of the impossibly pared-down furniture, I get on the travelator and revel in the Armani bookstore on the top floor, a fine way to counterbalance all that austerity downstairs.

Corso Como

Corso Como 10, 20154 Milan;
+39 02 2900 2674;
10corsocomo.com

This shop is almost a tourist destination now, but the trick is to sneak upstairs for the interiors and photography books. Just wonderful!

Spazio Rossana Orlandi

Via Matteo Bandello 14–16,
20123 Milan; +39 02 467 4471;
rossanaorlandi.com/lospazio

I find it hard to write about this shop because it's *so amazing*. Rossana Orlandi is the undisputed queen of style and every corner of her store offers style in spades. This and Merci are *the* best shops in the universe. If I had my last shopping day on earth, I'd go to both immediately. Dramatic, I know, but true.

L'Oro dei Farlocchi

Via Madonnina Fronte 5,
20121 Milan; +39 02 860 589;
lorodeifarlocchi.com

This place is incredible for antiques and art deco investment pieces. Top-end stuff, perfect for when you're feeling flush or you've just had a surprisingly good tax return. Ouch, but a good ouch.

Skitsch

Via Monte di Pietà 11, 20121 Milan;
+39 02 3663 3065; skitsch.it

Modernists and design junkies love this store. Skitsch is like a retail museum of all things designer and in a great part of town. It's loud and largely trend driven, but gives a good insight into what's happening in the world of product and furniture design.

Triennale di Milano

Viale Alemagna 6, 20121 Milan;
+39 02 724 341; triennale.it

If you have time, the Triennale, the museum of Italian design, is worth a quick visit. It reflects Milan's serious attitude to design.

It's probably irresponsible not to mention food when it comes to Milan. Here are some recommendations from the magnificent David Prior, my former assistant, now a bon vivant and food specialist. I've been to them all and I promise you won't be disappointed.

Da Giacomo

Via Pasquale Sottocorno 6, 20129
Milan; +39 02 7602 3313

Old-style Milanese baroque grandeur. On any given night you could spot Thomas Maier, Franca Sozzani or Lapo Elkann.

La Madonnina

Via Gentilino 6, 20136 Milan;
+39 02 8940 9089

Simple, cheap, quirky good food near the cool Navigli district.

Café Trussardi

Piazza della Scala 5, 20121 Milan;
+39 02 8068 8295;
trussardiallascala.com

This is a seriously beautiful glass box next to La Scala. It's well known, but possibly a touch too well known, so go here only for *aperitivi* and then race off somewhere else for dinner.

Bar Basso

Via Plinio 39, 20129 Milan;
+39 02 2940 0580; barbasso.com

Expect bow-tied waiters and Italy's top negroni.

New York

(Okay, okay, this is more than one day's worth, but it's New York, so I felt I was allowed a blowout!)

Kate Spade

454 Broome St, New York, NY 10013;
+1 212 274 1991; katespade.com

I'm a Kate Spade fan (even though the Spades have sold to the Liz Claiborne Group), so I always start with a visit to her finest store, which is still impossibly cute.

Kiosk

95 Spring St, New York, NY 10012;
+1 212 226 8601; kioskkiosk.com

I then head straight here to counter the polish and prep of Kate Spade. This incredible store undergoes a transformation every time its owner returns from her most recent travels. I've seen her take on Denmark, Mexico, America and Japan, and trust me, it's amazing.

Tinsel Trading

1 West 37th St, New York,
NY 10018; +1 212 730 1030;
tinseltrading.com

Buy up on cards, flowers, folly and more – it's chock full of surprises. Not an interiors store at all, more just dead good fun.

Clio

92 Thompson St, New York,
NY 10012; +1 212 966 8991;
clio-home.com

If you love dressing the table, Clio presents pieces from Toyko to Turkey within its handsome cupboards and hutches, which are also for sale – along with teapots, carafes, glassware and so much more.

Ochre

426 Broome St, New York,
NY 10013; +1 212 414 4332;
ochrestore.com

Ochre's offerings are soft, tactile and understated, in a considered palette of colours, with artisanal pieces alongside textiles, bedding and tabletop items.

Aero

419 Broome St, New York,
NY 10013; +1 212 966 4700;
aerostudios.com

Thomas O'Brien is the epitome of classic modern American style and it's easy to see why he's America's favourite tastemaker. His store is so great, just so great. Aero champions a gentle kind of warm modernism. Expect small objects as well as large room set-ups that will have you rethinking your living room. (He also designs a cheaper range, Modern Vintage, for the Target chain. It's worth the trip to 139 Flatbush Ave, Brooklyn if you're a die-hard fan.)

Paula Rubenstein Ltd

65 Prince St, New York,
NY 10012;
+1 212 966 8954

This is rich territory – nothing here is throwaway, it's all blue-blood and beautiful. Paula's stock is most collectable and covetable, largely thanks to her incredible eye. Beware, though, most people buy a piece, take it home and wonder why it doesn't look as good as it did in Paula's store. It's just that kind of place – dreamy.

ABC Home

888 Broadway, New York,
NY 10003; +1 212 473 3000;
abchome.com

This ten-floor landmark building is plainly and simply a great way to see the latest interior looks and trends. ABC merchandises really well and you can just suck it all in without feeling you must make a token purchase. If you feel so inclined, however, the price points range from small change in the trinket/paper section to big bucks for the furniture upstairs.

Moss

150 Greene St, New York,
NY 10012; +1 212 204 7100;
mossonline.com

I like to send first-time visitors to Moss as it's a great way to acquaint them with New York shopping.

Takashimaya

693 Fifth Ave, New York,
NY 10022; +1 212 350 0100;
takashimaya-ny.com

Meryl Streep in *The Hours* did her flower shopping here, remember? It's a zen experience, both exquisite and spare. I like to duck in to dodge the sensory overload that is Fifth Avenue. Expect no bargains (you have Tinsel Trading for that), just garden, home, bath and fashion accessories that are both minimal and luxe.

What Comes Around Goes Around

351 West Broadway, New York,
NY 10013; +1 212 343 1225;
nyvintage.com

This is vintage at its best – truly impressive rare items. Go there if you love to chase interesting objects and are feeling flush.

Partners and Spade

40 Great Jones St, New York,
NY 10012; +1 646 861 2827;
partnersandspade.com

Andy Spade (Kate's man) has set up, with creative collaborators, what I think is one of the cleverest stores in Manhattan. While it's really a front for their creative office, it is open to the public. I guarantee you'll walk out of there with a spring in your step, believing again in one-off merchants.

Antony Todd

44 East 11th St, New York,
NY 10003; +1 212 529 3252;
antonytodd.com

This Australian expat is the master of the Big Apple. Disciplined and beautiful, it's more showroom than store, but Antony's eye is second to none.

John Derian

6 East Second St, New York,
NY 10003; +1 212 677 3917;
johnderian.com

I hate to play favourites, but this is it. Who can resist the alphabet plates or whimsical paperweights? John's furniture for Cisco Brothers is incredibly beautiful, and he wears his heart on his store's sleeve. John Derian, you are an outstanding specimen of interior goodness!

Gramercy Park Hotel

2 Lexington Ave, New York,
NY 10010; +1 212 920 3300;
gramercyparkhotel.com

I love artist Julian Schnabel's fit-out of this majestic hotel. No need to stay (unless you aren't afraid of top room rates in US dollars) – a mooch around the lobby is satisfying enough.

Tokyo

I've asked Ebony Bizys to open her little black book for me here. I felt that the Tokyo listings needed to be super-recent (these guys make lightning-speed changeovers), and given her spot at the *Vogue Living* art desk and her adorable daily blog (hellosandwich. blogspot.com) – a love letter to all things design and Tokyo – she is by far the best person for the job.

Baden Baden

2-31-7 Chuocho, Meguro-ku
Tokyo 152-0001; +81 3 5722 3779;
badenbaden.jp

A gorgeous little shop set in an old house full of wonderful homewares, furniture and zakka.

Loft

21-1 Udagawacho, Shibuya-ku, Tokyo
150-0042; +81 3 3462 3807;
loft.co.jp/shop/shibuya

Amazing, amazing, amazing! My favourite department store in Tokyo is an oldie but a goodie. Pick up anything from gingham kotatsu cushions to furoshiki, Japanese tableware and mini-me Tokyo apartment furniture – basically everything you could ever need to set up (a super-cute) home in Tokyo.

Muji

3-8-3 Marunouchi, Chiyoda-ku,
Tokyo 100-0005; +81 3 5208 8241;
mujiyurakucho.com

We all know and love Muji but this is the biggest Muji store in the world. A two-storey pre-fab Muji house is set up inside the store, and there's a gallery space. They also stock some non-Muji items you won't find elsewhere.

Wasalaby

Colline Jiyugaoka, 2-9-19 Jiyugaoka
Meguro-ku, Tokyo 152-0035;
+81 3 3717 9191; wasalaby.com

Pick up gorgeous Japanese tableware. Great for gifts for friends back home.

Collex

1-1-4 Aobadai, Meguro-ku, Tokyo
153-0042; +81 3 57849 5612;
collex.jp

This is a team of two shops just down the road from one another (one more for interior accessories and the other more for furniture). Expect ceramics, furniture, graphic-design pieces and a collection of other quirky goods thrown in for good measure.

Cïbone

2-17-8 Jiyugaoka, Meguro-ku,
Tokyo 152-0035; +81 3 5729 7160;
cibone.com

This is *the* cutting-edge interior shop in Tokyo, completely ahead of its time. Think Moooi, Maarten Baas and those quirky kids at Committee.

Idée

2-16-29 Jiyugaoka, Meguro-ku,
Tokyo 154-0035; +81 3 5431 5720;
idee.co.jp

Fancy yourself living in a Japanese-style apartment? Try Idée for beautiful minimalist furniture, homewares and interior accessories. You'll want to move into the shop!

Saya

9-7-4 Akasaka, Minato-ku, Tokyo
107-8643; +81 3 5413 0709;
shop-saya.com

This cute shop in the Tokyo Midtown shopping centre sells Sori Yanagi homewares. (There are some other interiors shops on the same floor in Tokyo Midtown, so you can make a morning of it.)

LANTERN

Published by the Penguin Group
Penguin Group (Australia)
250 Camberwell Road, Camberwell, Victoria 3124, Australia
(a division of Pearson Australia Group Pty Ltd)
Penguin Group (USA) Inc.
375 Hudson Street, New York, New York 10014, USA
Penguin Group (Canada)
90 Eglinton Avenue East, Suite 700, Toronto, Canada ON M4P 2Y3
(a division of Pearson Penguin Canada Inc.)
Penguin Books Ltd
80 Strand, London WC2R 0RL England
Penguin Ireland
25 St Stephen's Green, Dublin 2, Ireland
(a division of Penguin Books Ltd)
Penguin Books India Pvt Ltd
11 Community Centre, Panchsheel Park, New Delhi – 110 017, India
Penguin Group (NZ)
67 Apollo Drive, Rosedale, North Shore 0632, New Zealand
(a division of Pearson New Zealand Ltd)
Penguin Books (South Africa) (Pty) Ltd
24 Sturdee Avenue, Rosebank, Johannesburg 2196, South Africa

Penguin Books Ltd, Registered Offices: 80 Strand, London, WC2R 0RL, England

First published by Penguin Group (Australia), 2010

1 3 5 7 9 10 8 6 4 2

Text copyright © Megan Morton 2010

The moral right of the author has been asserted

Design © Penguin Group (Australia)
Front cover photograph © Anthea Williamson
Back cover photograph © Trine Thorsen/Red Cover
Typeset in 12/16 Adobe Garamond by Post Pre-press Group
Colour reproduction by Splitting Image Colour Studio Pty Ltd, Clayton, Victoria
Printed and bound in China by 1010 Printing International Ltd

National Library of Australia
Cataloguing-in-Publication data:

Morton, Megan.
Home love / Megan Morton.
9781921382178 (hbk.)
Includes index.
Interior decoration.
747

penguin.com.au

acknowledgements

I love working with people cleverer than me. I thank all of those with whom I've had the good fortune to work closely, most notably Samantha Miller, Stephanie Blake, David Prior, Emma Elizabeth, Sara Silm and Emily Tayler. All clever cookies. Speaking of clever, a gracious thankyou to Julie Gibbs for getting HOME LOVE right from the start. Photographs copyright © William Abranowicz/Snapper Media (pp. 21, 25); Justin Alexander (pp. 117, 133); Jan Baldwin/Loupe Images (p. vi); Johnny Bouchier/Red Cover (p. 77); Hallie Burton (pp. 145, 165, 203); Jason Busch (pp. 11, 31, 69, 83, 141, 143, 151, 161, 169); Chris Chen (p. 3); B. Claessens/Inside/Picture Media (p. 127); Alexander Craig (p. 139); Grey Crawford (and Orlando Diaz-Azcuy)/Red Cover (p. 23); Tim Evan-Cook/Red Cover (p. 197); Grant Govier/Red Cover (p. 179); Per Gunnarson (p. 89); Reto Guntli/zapaimages.com (pp. 47, 85); Winifred Heinze/Red Cover (pp. 73, 193); Inside/H&L/Picture Media (p. 125); Inside/Picture Media (p. 51); Tim James (pp. 5, 9, 15, 29, 45, 107, 147); Juicy images (p. 149); Loupe Images/Ryland Peters & Small (pp. 13, 19, 43, 59, 75, 79, 87, 97, 123, 129, 131, 157, 163, 171, 201); Geoff Lung (p. 37, 53, 55, 61, 119, 135, 153); Geoff Lung with designaddict.com (p. 71); Geoff Lung with domusfurniture.co.uk (p. 91); Geoff Lung with emilyburningham.com (p. 81); Geoff Lung with Osborne & Little (p. 137); Geoff Lung with squintlimited.com (p. 93); Ray Main/Mainstream Images (pp. 17, 33, 39, 95, 151); Simon McBride/Red Cover (pp. 105, 191); Paul Massey/Mainstream Images (p. 181); Paul Massey/Red Cover (pp. 185, 173); Ngoc Minh Ngo (pp. 27, 99, 101, 103, 199); Marcus Peel/1st Option Representation (p. 63); Paul Raeside/Mainstream Images (p. 65); Ed Reeves/Red Cover (p. 121); Paul Ryan-Goff/Red Cover (p. 187); Anson Smart (pp. 35, 115, 113, 195); Trine Thorsen/Red Cover (p. 175); Debbie Treloar/Red Cover (p. 155); Chris Tubbs/Red Cover (p. 167); Michael Wee (pp. 57, 115, 167, 189); Anthea Williamson (p. 183); Mel Yates/Red Cover (p. 67)